How to Raise
Good Parents

How to Raise Good Parents

All Parents Are Born, Good Parents Are Developed

Lin Warmsley

Foreword by Mary D. Feduccia, PhD.

Cover and text illustrations by David Norwood
unless otherwise indicated

Design by Laura Gleason

ISBN-10: 148414130X
ISBN-13: 9781484141304

In loving memory of my parents,
who gave me the foundation to be the person I have become.

In memory of my beloved sister and brother
who sacrificed and dedicated their lives to the emotional,
cognitive, and physical development of their children.

To my sons
who taught me to understand
the fundamental meaning of the word
PARENTING—letter by letter;
who taught me that parenting
is a natural creative process defined and
continuously redefined through common parenting practices
combined with personalized parenting strategies;
but above all parenting is about the memories,
the applications, the experiences
as well as the heartaches and witnessing
the extraordinary fruits of my labor.

Special Acknowledgements

Mary D. Feduccia, Ph.D. for her extraordinary
marathon guidance and boundless support
of my parenting profile and project.
From 1992 until now, Mary has been my cheerleader and
confidante. Thank you is not enough.

Ryan Buxton and Emma Morel
Your energy matched my enthusiasm;
your dedication matched my allegiance.
Together we were the alpha and the omega.
Thank you for your contribution—this is it.
Mission accomplished!

And
meet the crew
(the development committee)
Roy W. Lester, Jerry Tim Brooks, Sybil Taylor Holt, and
Stan Lewis; Coach Elton, Barbara and Elnita Blount;
Cedric Patin, Lance Jackson, (the late) Les Roberts,
Calloway's Gym, Amateur Athletic Union (AAU)
and the Sports Academy; Sister Patricia Sullivan (ret),
Fathers (the late) Kenneth Smith and Francis Ferrier (ret),
Anne Marks, Raymond and Dorothy Calendro;
Priscilla Burkhalter, Stephanie Remson, and Jamie Hayes.
Family is a community affair!

Contents

Contents

Contents

Foreword

Mary D. Feduccia, Ph.D.
Baton Rouge, Louisiana

Ever feel like you haven't yet discovered the fantastic parent inside yourself? Ever wish you had an instruction manual to guide you to becoming the type of parent who will make an everlasting positive impact on your sons and daughters? Ever thought about developing a parent book to document your parenting experiences, goals, and milestones like the baby book you probably developed after each of your children entered the world?

If you answered "yes" to any of these questions, the book you are holding was written for you! Lin Warmsley has created an interactive workbook that illustrates step-by-step how to parent your children effectively to prepare them for success in the 21st century. Her overarching goal is to help parents like you raise strong adults who have learned from you to stand on their own and live their lives based on the values you have instilled within them. Lin is a parenting strategist and family researcher who successfully raised three children as a single parent.

Her book is based on grounded research on parenting, interviews with parents, and personal experiences in her own parenting journey. Realizing quite some time ago that *parenting is a job too,* Lin developed a project to lead and guide parents to understand what makes people tick and how we can all harness our own natural parenting abilities to raise a wonderful child. This book is the first in her three-part series to change the mindset of parents about how they can nurture and strengthen their natural parenting abilities to help their children discover their purpose in life.

Over our many years of collaboration, Lin has inspired me and impressed me as one of the absolutely most effective parents I've ever had the privilege of working with. She discovered early on that parenting each of her three sons required different parenting skills and styles, depending on each child's personality, goals, performance, and other factors—learning from each child then improving and modifying on the next child's development. I worked most closely with her second son, Titus, as his high school guidance counselor.

Titus was a star on the school's basketball team and aspired to play at the college and professional levels. He faced the uphill struggle of needing to achieve a certain ACT score much higher than his first score to obtain a scholarship to his first-choice college and to play basketball. I've worked with thousands of high school and college students over the past 35 years and never met anyone who exceeded Titus in drive, motivation, perseverance, and the ability to deal with defeat, while on a remarkable journey to achieving his goals.

I'll never forget the day he received his ACT report with a score above what he needed for the scholarship. He bounded into my office, jumped so high he nearly touched the ceiling, and expressed deep gratitude for my help and guidance, and that of his teachers and coaches, but most of all, his mom.

In *How to Raise Good Parents* Lin provides the framework and a strong foundation for you to be a phenomenal parent and to realize at a very deep and meaningful level what being a parent means to you. In this customized guide, she leads you through nine chapters using the acronym P-A-R-E-N-T-I-N-G to help you:

- Build your child's self-knowledge
- Encourage self-regulation
- Promote personal development
- Understand the skills needed to position your child in the marketplace
- Realize the value of developing relationships and nurturing social connections as well as fostering empathy.
- Track child's development culminating as a high school graduation heirloom given to child to continue building on his/her self-mastery.

She uses anecdotes from her own experience as a parent to make the concepts applicable to all parents and young people who are growing strong on their own. She provides specific steps in each chapter to apply the concepts and integrate them into your day-to-day parenting. At the end of each chapter is a *Ways To* section, which briefly summarizes the chapter, provides tips on how to execute, and master the suggested skills along with supplemental resources such as related books, movies and songs that will inspire you and your children.

Additionally, *Tell Your Story* at the end of each chapter provides the opportunity to reflect on what's happened to you, how you've been parented, how you'd like to parent, and how these factors hugely influence your parenting style. Telling your story is an important way of processing the information in each chapter and personalizing it, something that most parents don't find the time to do amid the hustle and bustle of daily life.

Lin shares her challenges and how she survived them as a single mother, often not knowing whether to buy milk or put gas in her car. Her inspirational approach to parenting and to life as a whole is directed to parents of children of all ages, including special sections on parenting young teens, college-age sons and daughters, and children who have become parents themselves.

Whether you are thinking about and hoping to be a parent, are feeling that as a parent you're in a new career with no training, or are simply motivated to be the best parent or youth guardian you can be, Lin's book has relevance and great value for you. She shares a *Legacy Library* with you in the form of her favorite books, movies, and music that reinforce the parenting guidance provided in earlier sections of the book. They provide excellent vehicles for discussion with your children to reinforce the lessons you want to teach and the values you hope to ingrain.

Lin is a master at creating mental messages through "motivational quotes" such as, "If you see yourself as a giant, you will act like one," and "Parenting has not changed; society has." This book will unequivocally equip you with the knowledge, skills, and inspiration to unlock the fantastic parent inside of you and to help you relish parenting as one of the most important things you can do for your children. As Lin so wisely points out, "All parents are born; good parents are developed." Now is your time to develop into the amazing parent you were meant to be!

Mary D. Feduccia, Ph.D., LPC
Baton Rouge, Louisiana

Introduction

Parenting: A Life's Endeavor

People often say that parenting comes without instructions; however, I have created this mini parenting guide to serve as just that. This guide is a customized workbook and the first of a three-part personal parenting manual. It is designed to offer support and assistance in your parenting journey, as well as provide you with a place to document your family's experiences, stories, and beliefs.

All of my life's work—from academia to parenting—has led me to this project. Initially, my goal was to learn to document how to become a good parent and develop outstanding children by attempting to understand what it means to be a parent. My second goal was to share developmental parenting anecdotes—essentially about my experiences with my own children, as I helped them understand themselves and their own journeys from birth to adulthood.

The content in this guide is based on interviews and first-hand experiences with parents of all ages. It breaks down the word "parenting" in a meaningful, easy to remember way, which allows you to have an active role in the reading experience. The book offers my own experiences, and those of others, as guides to assess and improve your own parenting skills.

We will take this journey together. This book will allow you to incorporate and develop your personal parenting strategy by offering a parenting plan based on common practices and providing support and guidance on your journey to becoming a successful parent.

Each chapter allows you to make personal parenting notes reflecting on both your own childhood and current parenting experiences. It is a valuable story—a treasure—that you document for each child, detailing his/her developmental stages and assets as well as struggles and challenges, resulting in a customized parenting journal that you can pass down to your children. Imagine that!

Throughout this work, I primarily focused on six areas which I believe are important to keep in mind at all times:

- Encouraging self-awareness and self-regulation
- Encouraging personal development
- Understanding and identifying skills needed to position your child in the marketplace
- Understanding how to develop relationships and nurture social connections
- Promoting empathy
- Keeping a journal of one's journey as a parent (this book can be a keepsake and a unique high school gift to each child)

This book serves two purposes: to assist and guide your journey as a parent and to document your own parenting journey so that your children may have a strong foundation to look back on and grow from when they become parents. It is my hope that you will connect your own stories with mine and develop your own accounts with the goal of developing your children to become good parents.

In the movie *The Help*, the women reminded me of my own

mother who not only took care of her home and children, but cleaned the homes of other women and raised their children as well. The visual image of those women validated and motivated me to be strong and persevere through any peril to raise good men.

I took matters into my own hands, and I did things on my own terms. As a result, I wrote my story and defined my family. *So can you.* The key to parenting success is to write your story before society writes it for you.

Share with Me

I would like to hear from you. Please *tell me your stories* as well *as* which of my *personal stories* impacted you and how you plan to apply them to your family. Also, please share your own customized parenting strategies designed to fit your family's needs. I also invite you to contribute to my next series *Parenting: It's a Job Too!*

Email me at powerfulparenting97@gmail.com

Children Learn What They Live

—Dorothy Law Neite

If a child lives with **criticism**, he learns to **condemn**.

If a child lives with **hostility**, he learns to **fight**

If a child lives with **ridicule**, he learns to be **shy**.

If a child lives with **shame**, he learns to feel **guilty**.

If a child lives with **tolerance**, he learns to be **patient**.

If a child lives with **encouragement,** he learns **confidence.**

If a child lives with **praise**, he learns to **appreciate**.

If a child lives with **fairness**, he learns **justice**.

If a child lives with **security**, he learns to have **faith**.

If a child lives with **approval**, he learns to **like** himself.

If a child lives with **acceptance and friendship**,
he learns to **find love** in the world.

What Does Parenting Really Mean?

Being a parent is many things, but what does
the word "parenting" actually mean,
and how can mothers and fathers use the word
to assess their own performances?

This interactive guide dissects the word "parenting"
and uses a mix of research, family interviews, and
anecdotes from Lin's own life as a single mother of three
to develop a step-by-step, letter-by-letter approach
to developing great kids.
There is a fantastic parent within us all,
and the map to realizing that potential
is built right into this nine-letter word:
PARENTING

Part One

Letter by Letter:
P-A-R-E-N-T-I-N-G

Parents are many things:
teachers, nurses, chefs, coaches, mentors,
playmates, chauffeurs, and the list goes on.
But we need to find out what
being a parent means at its core.
We'll do this by carefully analyzing the
word "parenting" and finding
what the word tells us
about what our children need.

> *"A family that prays together stays together."*
>
> —Unknown

Chapter 1

P: PRAYER

No one has all the answers. This is the first rule of both parenting and life in general. When our children are young, they look to us for guidance when they don't know what to do. But just as we learned that our own parents are only human, there will come a time when our children need a sense of absolute security that no one person can offer. It's a feeling that can come only from **prayer.**

Although we do our best as parents to provide our children with as many answers as possible, we are only human, and unfortunately, we do not have all the answers. When in doubt, we can turn to God. Prayer should be the focal point of the family unit. It's the string that binds parents and children together for a flourishing spiritual existence.

Teach children that prayer is not just the antidote to life's challenges, but also the key to reaching alignment with a power superior to us. We should pray when things are wrong, but we should also pray when things are right, when we feel gratitude, and when we need to make tough decisions. Surround your children with prayer from the start so they know where to look when they need direction they can't get from you or anyone else.

Prayer, like religion, is rife with mystery, but that's what *faith* is all about—*trusting* a force that we can't see but that we know is there. Due to the mysterious qualities of prayer and children's natural curiosity, they will surely approach parents with questions about the family's faith. Here are a few of the myriad questions they may ask: Why do we pray? How do we know if there really is a superior being? Why is it important to live a spiritual existence? These questions are important, and as parents, we must directly confront them rather than deflecting the inquiries.

Children's instinctual curiosity creates questions about prayer and faith. They're learning about the world around them at a rate more rapid than they will ever experience again. Instead of assuming their questions are fueled by doubt or rebelliousness, use their questions as teachable moments to explore faith with your child. Explain how you arrived at your faith and why you believe what you do. This is your chance to show your children the path to spiritual nourishment.

While guiding your children in their faith is important and necessary, don't be afraid to let your children explore their own beliefs. Rather than force-feeding your own faith, give your children the freedom to develop their own experience. Religion is personal, and the most we can do as parents is introduce our beliefs, explain why they work for us, and let our children find their way to spirituality in their own time.

Personal Story

I Need You Lord

School Night

After working a night shift during his senior year of high school, my son Marcus fell asleep at the wheel and rear-ended an 18-wheeler. The car slid under the trailer of the truck, and the windshield and roof were completely flattened, and smashed into the car. The scene of the wreck looked fatal; however, he survived. He told me he was saved by someone more powerful than he—if it weren't for God, he wouldn't have survived.

Summer Time

Four years later, Titus was involved in a car wreck shortly after graduating high school. Again, my son fell asleep at the wheel, and he veered off the road and hit another vehicle parked on the side of the interstate. When he came home, he said, "Mama, I shouldn't be here today, but I guess it just wasn't my time. I could only think of one person who saved me from death. It was God." He went on to tell me how grateful he was to have his life spared so he could continue to strive for and fulfill his goals in life.

College Experience

Towards the end of Julius's senior year of college, expenses were quickly mounting. We were discussing upcoming events and expenses, and Julius realized he had a car insurance payment due soon as well. I told him, "Don't worry, I'll handle it."

Before ending our conversation, we agreed that we should not worry because God always works things out.

After hanging up, I walked outside to check the mail, and there was a letter for Julius containing a check for $325.00. I called Julius and asked him who sent him a check for this money and why? He said, "She was my landlady, and the check is the deposit she owed me." I informed him I had deposited the check in the bank, and his car insurance payment was taken care of. We both laughed and together said, "God is good," and I ended with "and on time all the time."

Using this incident as a teachable moment, I told him, "Let this encounter show you miracles come in small doses, and always put your trust in God."

Kids Will Be Kids

Reflecting on these stories reminded me of a similar heavenly experience when I was ten years old. Similar to Titus and Marcus, my life was saved by divine intervention when someone threw a brick into a window I was standing near. The neighborhood children and I were playing outside, and some other children decided to start throwing rocks at us. We moved inside, but the rock throwing continued and escalated. All of the other children went home, but I stood fast outside the window, determined to stand my ground. One of the children picked up a large brick, and hurled it at the window, aiming directly at my forehead.

Right before the brick made impact, someone yelled, "Lin, duck!" I felt a shove and tumbled to the ground. Once things settled down, I looked around, and no one was there. I knew then it was an angel sent from God, and from that day forward, I have been so thankful to God for his divine intervention and have vowed to share my story with others.

There have been so many painful encounters in my family, but we are always rescued by a being more powerful than us. I continue to teach my children never to doubt the power of God, nor forget their spiritual foundation. Together, we work to build a close relationship with God, and we trust in Him to stand by us during our difficult days and guide us toward fulfillment and happiness.

Personal Story

Walk by Faith, Not by Sight
by Kendric Smith

"For I know the plans I have for you, declares the Lord,
"plans to prosper you and not to harm you,
plans to give you hope and a future."
—Jeremiah 29:11

When it came to playing football, I felt at times that I was handed the short end of the stick. In my junior year of high school, I struggled. While most of my classmates were gearing up to play on the varsity team, I was on the junior varsity squad. However, in my senior year I earned a starting role—playing in every game. That year, at every game, I wore the church's motto on a necklace that stated, "It's favor time in 2009."

That year, I felt the presence of God and I thanked Him for my bishop's vision of excelling in the game which encouraged me to do my best. I did! By the end of the football season, I led the tight ends in the district's receptions. What a great way to end my senior year!

Because of my success on the football field, my family and I had high expectations of my receiving a Division 1 (D1) football scholarship. However, though colleges expressed interest, they did not offer me a scholarship. Even though my heart was set on a football scholarship, I did not place all my eggs in one basket. I also applied for a ROTC scholarship.

So, when The United States Army offered me an ROTC scholarship to Utah State University or Louisiana State University (LSU), I accepted, attending LSU. I also joined the LSU football team as a walk on. Although my goal in high school was not to walk on to a football team, it was my only option. LSU was known throughout the Southeastern Conference (SEC) as one of the best football programs in the nation.

My first year at LSU was rough. The obligations of academics, football, and ROTC were overwhelming. I was not physically nor mentally prepared for so many demands. Those challenges hindered my success in football, ROTC, and above all academics. My situation was spiraling out of control. I was on a journey, unclear about my true destination, but at least I was doing something.

Even though I was panicking and did not know how to survive my circumstances, God knew. God stayed faithful to me. He already had a plan in motion. My growing love for football and ROTC became a major dilemma, but I decided to give up ROTC.

At the end of the spring semester, I returned home to Texas. In late July, I decided to enroll at Blinn Community College where I could further pursue my dream of playing football. However, when I arrived at Blinn, I still had to fight for a spot on the team. Once again, I faced challenges because Blinn had started football practice for the approaching season two weeks before I got there. Not only that, I was embarrassed for leaving a great institution, LSU, but Blinn Community College gave me a chance. My family and I were grateful.

As I set short and long term goals, I prayed to God to lead and guide me. One of my goals was to continue my journey to a Division 1 school. I asked God to allow me to graduate from Blinn by the end of the school year. I also asked God to help me succeed not only in academics but in football at Blinn. Shortly thereafter, my coaches and teammates recognized and complimented my athleticism, conviction, and knowledge of the game.

My thoughts returned to my dream of playing at the D1 level but my feelings faded when I learned about the NCAA transfer rule. Because I was the sixth transfer, and only five transfer students were eligible to play, I would not be allowed to play my first year.

I was discouraged because being ineligible for the 2011/2012 season would make it impossible for me to be recruited by D1 universities. However, I was determined; I stayed true to my goals; I kept my faith in God while maintaining a 3.45 GPA. In one academic year, I crammed in 40 credits hours. While at LSU, my academics took a hit, so this academic achievement was a blessing.

On May 10, 2012, I graduated from Blinn with an associate degree in social science. I was happy; my family was happy. Mission accomplished, but I had no idea where I would be attending school in the fall of 2012.

Shortly after graduation, I wrote a petition to God with the scripture Habakkuk 2:2-4 written out. My petition expressed the desires of my heart. Daily, I stood in faith, thanking, believing, and trusting in God that my goals would be fulfilled. I knew my effort meant growing spiritual maturity and drew me closer to God. Therefore, I continued to pray for a D1 scholarship and wasn't going to stop until I got it!

Then it happened. In the midst of my spiritual journey, D1 recruiters started calling and one school stood out the most. After emailing Ohio University and receiving timely, consistent, and interested responses, I knew God had his hands on me and it was his will when one of the Ohio football coaches happened to be in my area. We arranged to meet.

Unknowingly and needless to say, I was on a journey and God knew my destination. God instilled in me the desire to attend and play defense for Blinn. During my faith walk along the way, God's plan was moving me closer to my dream. However, God wanted me to be doing something until it was time for me to receive his blessing. Who knew the when, the why, and the how of it all?

The Ohio University football program offered me a scholarship and the opportunity to play defense but I had to fight for a starting position as a defensive end. My spiritual walk took a few more weeks of constant prayer of thankfulness and gratefulness. Then on June 6, 2012, I achieved my dream. I signed a D1 football scholarship with Ohio University.

Many people doubted my efforts and dreams. They said I could not reach this goal without recent football film, especially so late in my collegiate football career. Nevertheless, I kept my faith and belief in myself, and God saw the best in me and He blessed me.

I thanked God for the prayer partners and support systems that encouraged and assisted me in reaching my goals and dreams. I want to encourage my fellow brothers and sisters to align their goals with the will of God.

Trust me, when you stand your ground with God's words and your convictions, God will do what is good for you and you will prosper. He will fulfill the desires and the provisions of your heart. I thank God for taking me through this faith walk to spiritual maturity. He taught me how to depend on him.

My dreams might be different from yours but be encouraged to write down your vision and make a plan that includes strengthening your faith in God. His spiritual journey is to prepare you for his will and when you are ready, he will fulfill his promise and always be there for you.

Where Is Kendric Now?

Recently, I spoke with Kendric's mother. Deborah told me that Kendric graduated with honors from Ohio University in Organizational Communications and is currently working with Dell computer in Texas. Kendric and his family continue to walk by faith with God's Favor.

Supplemental Resources

- Suggested listening: "Never Would Have Made It" by Marvin Sapp
- Suggested reading: *The Bible, Wild at Heart* by John Eldredge, *The Power of the Praying Parent* and *The Power of Praying for Your Adult Children* by Stormie Omartian
- Suggested viewing: *War Room* and *Woodlawn*

Personal Story
Finding My Way Back Home
The Travis Mott Story

I'll start with my favorite disclaimer: I love to get high but I hate being an active drug addict. I wish that I could have one and not the other, but that is impossible, they are both one and the same. If I am going to commit the crime then I must be ready to do the time.

I believe that I was born with an addictive predisposition. Long before my first hit, I could never settle for the status quo. Regardless of the circumstances, whatever I had or did always had to be one cut above the rest. Bigger, faster, and stronger than the accepted standard was exactly what I wanted or aspired to be. Needless to say, I was insatiable from the get-go.

Growing up I never experienced a life in a broken home, I was never physically, verbally, or sexually abused, and nothing traumatizing ever really occurred in my life. With a healthy upbringing, I could never point a finger at an incident that would justify my behavior. I drank and I drugged essentially because I liked the effect produced by the substance at hand.

As an adolescent, I had heard much talk of Jesus; a man of love and strength. But what a man was two thousand years ago meant nothing to me, today. I could tell you that he existed, but trusting in him or living for him was the furthest thing from my agenda.

My first experience with dope was almost like a spiritual experience, but without God. (If such a thing were possible.) All of those feelings of inadequacy vanished and were replaced with an elusive feeling of being calm, confident, and collected. It truly did for me what nothing else could.

Life went on and my occasional habit became a full-fledged

dependency. When I tried to control it, I could not enjoy it, and at the same time whenever I could enjoy it, I could not control it. This bad habit took on a life of its own. Somewhere along the line my power of choice just seemed to evaporate. I was hooked. Drugs were not getting in the way of my life; it was more like my life was in the way of my drugs.

School, my parents, and the cops did not take too kindly to my lifestyle either. I remember many lectures, ultimatums, restrictions, expulsions, arrests, license suspensions, court dates, and incarcerations. I remember thinking, "God, grant me the power to change the people, places, and things that do not agree with my way of thinking."

Things became increasingly worse, never better. My relationship with my family was deteriorating day by day. I would steal money from them, pawn their belongings, and then offer to help look for them whenever they came up missing. My mother drifted into despondency and lost faith in me completely. It always seemed that no matter how distant, cold, or callous I became, listening to her cry always pierced me deep down to the very marrow in my bones. Countless times I would stand before my parents and tell them that I would quit, and I meant it with every fiber in my body. Sometimes I would last a day, if I was lucky, before I would be right back where I started.

After my first stay in rehab, my mother began to attend Al-Anon meetings. Whenever she came back from them it really interfered with my manipulation of her. I swore that it must have been 'self-esteem' day at their meeting or something of that nature. My father became my chief enabler after that, so I relied on him to keep a roof over my head and food in my stomach since my mother was beginning to develop a love for me that was gentle enough to let go.

Let it be known that peer pressure was nonexistent to me.

I never did a drug that I did not already want to do although mingling with some unscrupulous members of the community did not contribute to a solution. I was eventually introduced to intravenous heroin use. Temporarily, my problems would melt beneath me only to sprout back up sometimes worse than they were before. So I ended up where I swore I never would—as a junkie.

In the book of Proverbs, there is a verse which states, "Above all else, guard your heart, for it is the wellspring of life." Had I listened to that piece of wisdom, perhaps I may not have found myself as a living garbage receptacle for chemicals. The lens of my heart had become so distorted that I could not distinguish the true from the false, resulting in deep depression. I believe this verse places so much emphasis on watching what we allow in because God knows that to lose heart means to lose everything.

It was not until one day when the pain of change seemed preferable to the pain of staying the same that I took a step in the right direction. I admitted myself into a detoxification center for the second time to go through withdrawal. Coming off of that stuff was an absolute hell that I would not wish upon my worst enemy.

My father picked me up from that hospital and told me that I was no longer welcome home, and all that he would help me with financially was finding help. I could see that I had exhausted my resources and was at the end of my rope. To be honest, there was nothing noble or virtuous in my deciding to give recovery another shot. I only did it to save my own skin. I have heard it shared in meetings that all of us addicts were on the dump truck headed to the dump. Some could smell it coming so they jumped off while others just had to hang on and ride it all of the way. By God's grace coupled with pain and tough love, I smelled it coming and jumped off.

I moved back to Enid, Oklahoma into a sober living environment I had been in once before. I would be lying if I said that I've been tiptoeing through the tulips ever since. But in all honesty, my worse day sober does not hold a candle to my best day high. A broken heart and an open mind was all that was necessary to let my will come into agreement with God's will. People in the rooms of AA genuinely loved me until I could love myself. They gave of themselves unsparingly. I became involved in a church, rededicated my life to Christ by baptism, prayed, meditated on God's word, attended AA meetings, sought wise counsel, and studied the book of Alcoholics Anonymous.

The scalefrom my eyes were removed and I could see that I had been saved from a dead end future. I could now see that Jesus died for it, so that I did not have to die from it. In my darkest days he was right beside me just waiting to be called upon. Today I lean on his sustaining grace. Today I can see that he has kept and is continuing to keep his promise when he said that he has come to make all things new. Restoration has been a direct result of following the risen Christ.

Unfortunately, it took three trips to a treatment center, two detox clinics, two trips to a sober living environment, and a whole lot of my parents' money for me to learn this fundamental truth. What can I say? I am a slow learner.

It has been said that courage is not the same as bravery. To me, bravery is just something that people are born with. You either have it, or you do not. Courage, on the other hand, is far different. Courage is being deathly afraid, but following through with the thing that terrifies you anyway. I believe we are all capable of courage.

Today life has taken on an entirely new meaning. My family loves me and trusts me again. I take pride in my work. I've won the esteem of my colleagues. School is again a part of my life after I had dropped out my senior year. That feeling of impending doom has become a brighter vision of the future. Misery has become compassion. Apathy has become sincerity. Stories of sin have become stories that can help and heal others who are also afflicted. Today, I can give love without selfishness getting in the way. I can look people in the eye. I can experience a wide array of emotion. It is okay for me to cry sometimes. It is okay to feel again. I have meaningful relationships. My desire for a companion has been fulfilled. I have a beautiful girlfriend whom I love, respect, and adore. I am happy, joyous, and free. And the list goes on ad infinitum!

All these things have been granted to me over such a short stint of sobriety that it is downright bewildering. Had I been able to see the way that I live today back when I was still using, I would have said that I'd never treat myself that well. All it took was some honesty, open-mindedness, and willingness, and God has worked a miraculous change in my life. I am a person who has recovered from a seemingly hopeless condition of the mind and body. For that, I am eternally grateful.

I will end with a quote from O. R. Melling that I am rather fond of. In times of frustration, anxiety, and doubt I recall this declaration of faith: "When you come to the edge of all that you know, you must believe one of two things: either there will be ground to stand on, or you will be given wings to fly."

Supplemental Resources

- Suggested Listening: "Never Would Have Made It" by Marvin Sapp
- Suggested reading: *Beautiful Boy* by David Sheff
- Suggested viewing: *The Basketball Dairy*
- Suggested viewing: *War Room* and *Woodlawn*

The Good Morning God Prayer

Good Morning God!
You are ushering in another day,
untouched and freshly new.
So here I am to ask you, God,
you'll renew me too.
Forgive the many errors that I made yesterday
and let me try again dear God
to walk closer in your way.

But Lord, I am well aware;
I can't make it on my own.
So take my hand and hold it tight,
for I cannot walk alone.

http://www.catholic.org/news/hf/faith/story.php?id=67825

Evening Prayer

I adore Thee, my God,
and I love Thee with all my heart.

I give Thee thanks for having created me,
for having made me a Christian,
and for having preserved me this day.

Pardon me for the evil I have done today;
if I have done anything good, do Thou accept it.
Keep me while I take my rest
and deliver me from all dangers.

May Thy grace be always with me.

Amen.

http://www.catholic.org/news/hf/faith/story.php?id=67825

Ways To Incorporate ...

Prayer allows us to grow as adults and parents along with our children. Not only does prayer stimulate our spiritual existence, but it also teaches us the importance of observing, reflecting, teaching, and listening. Through family prayer, parents are given an incredible opportunity to instill a moral compass in their children. This compass will guide them in the right direction when they are grown and out of your direct care, providing peace of mind to both your children and you.

Here Are a Few Ways to Incorporate Spiritual and Mental Growth and Development for Your Family

- Use prayer cards to guide daily devotionals
- Show children how to find peace of mind through *meditation*
- Identify a special place of solitude at home
- Read Bible stories relating to the child's daily experiences
- Talk about how special things happened throughout the day's activities that reflect spiritual guidance
- Teach them miracles come in small packages
- Teach your children how to understand and listen to their gut feelings [God's way of speaking to us]
- Teach them to understand their natural power of instinct

Supplemental Resources

- Suggested reading: *The Bible*
- Suggested viewing: Check out https://www .spiritualcinemacircle.com/
- Suggested listening: "Stronger" by Mandisa, "Circle of Life" from Disney's *Lion King*, "We Believe" by the Newsboys, "Grandpa" by The Judds, and "Wait on the Lord" by Shirley Caesar

Tell Your Story:

_____

_____

_____

_____

_____

_____

_____

_____

_____

_____

_____

_____

_____

_____

_____

_____

_____

_____

_____

_____

_____

_____

_____

_____

_____

_____

_____

_____

_____

_____

_____

_____

_____

_____

_____

_____

_____

_____

P: Prayer

_____

_____

_____

_____

_____

_____

_____

_____

_____

_____

_____

_____

_____

_____

_____

_____

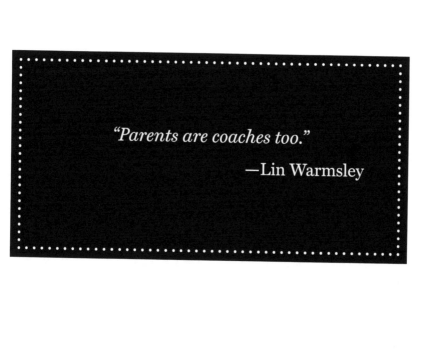

"Parents are coaches too."

—Lin Warmsley

Chapter 2

A: ADVOCATE AND ADVISOR

SELF-
ACTUALIZATION
Pursue Inner Talent
Creativity   Fullfilment

SELF-ESTEEM
Achievement Mastery
Recognition Respect

BELONGING - LOVE
Friends Family Spouse Lover

SAFETY
Security Stability Freedom from Fear

PHYSIOLOGICAL
Food Water Shelter Warmth

http://psed516diversityproject.wikispaces.com/Maslow's+
Hierarchy+of+Needs+in+an+Inclusion+Classroom-+By+Kaitlin+Lutz

A s in any job, the duties of a parent change over time. Just as an employee's responsibilities and projects develop as he or she grows into the work, a parent must allow their child-rearing strategies to evolve as children become adolescents and then adults. The psychologist Abraham Maslow explains this personal evolution in his "hierarchy of needs," which outlines the essential requirements for children to properly develop into self-assured, successful adults.

Parents must adapt with their children as these needs are met. In the very early stages of development, parents first meet a child's physical needs and provide love. As they grow, a parent serves as an **advocate,** and you play a critical role in decision making for your child/children. As your child becomes capable of making his/her own decisions, you transform to the role of an **advisor,** and rather than telling them what to do, you guide and advise them as they make their own decisions.

Parents advocate for their children as they climb the first rungs of Maslow's ladder. As a parent, your primary responsibility is the survival of your child, which Maslow declares in the first rung of the ladder. Secondly, as a parent, you should provide security and stability for your child because at this stage of life, your child is impressionable and uncertain of his/her place in the world. Children, at these early stages, need mothers and fathers who can recognize how to enhance their children's existence and provide a clear path for them to follow.

Advocacy is about protection—the "mama bear" instinct drives parents to take control of acquiring resources for children. Under your advocacy, children acquire the third level of Maslow's hierarchy: belonging and love. Your guidance teaches them their role in the family and community. This also lays the foundation for their future relationships, both romantic and platonic.

After laying this solid foundation for your children, your parenting role transitions from advocate to advisor, which allows them to conquer the final two rungs of Maslow's ladder—self-esteem and self-actualization. These final steps are all about independence. Your children must complete these steps themselves, independent of you. You will no longer take a proactive, forceful approach by doing things for your child. Instead, you will assume a more passive, advisory role.

This does not mean back away or become less involved in your children's lives; it just means trusting your child to rely on the foundation you have laid for him/her when making decisions. Your child now sees you as consultant and counselor, rather than commander. Your children will inevitably make mistakes and veer from prospective paths; however, with advice and input from you, they'll learn from every step.

Mindset and Mental Messages

"A Mind is a terrible thing to waste" (UNCF). In 1972, this slogan was developed by the United Negro College Fund. In my parenting practice, my goal was to shape the mindsets of my children as well as promote and preserve the following virtues: respectfulness, fair-mindedness, and accountability, and above all personal growth.

As a youth, the UNCF motto validated my desire to obtain a college degree and also the importance of brain development. Still today, 43 years later, this saying lingers in my mind and impacts my strategic approach to parenting.

Based on my sons' individual talents, personalities, and behaviors, I created passionate and enthusiastic acronyms and mental messages. These customized mentalities were designed to render support and positive reactions to day by day encounters and above all develop situational and adaptive leadership skills, which would be especially helpful to them when they were out on their own.

Throughout *How to Raise Good Parents,* you will learn how a few of the mentalities shaped the mindset of each child.

Acronyms

- B.E.D. **B**e Respectful; **E**njoy Being A Kid; **D**efine Your Role
- B.U.D. **B**e Respectful; **U**nderstand Self; **D**efine Your Role
- B.E.D. **B**e Respectful; **E**njoy Your Life; **D**efine Your Role
- L.C.D. your **L**ife; your **C**hoice; your **D**ecision

- P.A.C. **P**arents **A**re **C**oaches, too!
- G.R.P. **G**randparents **R**etirement **P**lan

Mentalities

- Find a way to make a play
- Philosophy: plan, prepare, pray; if you do your best, God will do the rest
- Trilogy of life: transition, turmoil, transformation
- Walk into a room like you own it . . . no one will know the difference
- Community is a family affair
- Respect is not an option; respect is a virtue
- Children are gifts to society; what's your contribution?
- Parenting has not changed . . . society has!
- Don't play house in my house
- I am your mother's eyes
- Your mother would be proud of you; yes, she raised you right
- My goal is to help you understand your tomorrow, today
- My intention is to help you reach your potential
- Education is not optional; education is an investment
- Don't settle, don't compete, set the standard, be the competition
- I got your back, don't put a target on mine
- My mom said I was creating myself; my grandmother had my brain scanned; mom was right!

Personal Story
"Parents are Coaches too"

I am a product of a Catholic education, and always intended the same for my children. After completing high school, I began to truly appreciate the discipline and routine instilled in me by my education. My goal for my children was not only to establish a strong religious foundation, but to help them understand the importance of education. Success in both of these arenas would ensure positive prospects for their futures.

When it was time for Julius to enter pre-school, I decided to place him with a friend of mine who was a teacher, and he stayed with her for two years. By the time he was ready for big boy school, a new performing arts school was opening. Julius loved to sing and dance, so I thought this school would be a fantastic fit for him. They also offered an extended day program for children who needed after hours care, which made it all the more appealing to me since I was not only working as an adjunct professor and working full time at the Department of Natural Resources, but also completing my doctoral studies.

The selection and admissions process was rigorous; however, by the middle of that school year, I learned my son was accepted! Mission accomplished!

After a year of academic hit and miss, I realized this school was not the best choice for Julius, and I reopened my investigation into schools to fit into his educational plan. After countless hours of research and many school visits, I found the perfect school for my son.

We encountered another rigorous admissions process, and we were relieved when Julius passed the entrance exam. However, the school's principal denied his entrance because she felt he was too active and would struggle to maintain self-discipline in the traditional classroom setting they offered. She suggested ADHD medication, but medication was simply not an option for me. I knew my son could do this on his own.

The following year, we reapplied. This time, I sought the support of the school's priest. Julius was accepted on the second attempt under the condition that he repeat the third grade. I succeeded in my mission to place my son in an environment that would spark his natural abilities, nurture and develop his character, sharpen and influence his leadership qualities, and provide support for the relationships he would create both at school and at home.

Five years later, he graduated with honors and received a one-time $1,500 Leadership Scholarship to the Catholic high school of his choice. Throughout his high school career, Julius was actively involved in junior military programs, and he thrived in that environment. From an early age, I noticed his physical strength and mental abilities as well as his need for structure and discipline, so I got him involved in programs like these at an early age, thinking he might pursue the military as a career option.

When he graduated from high school after a spectacular academic and athletic tenure, I was thrilled when he accepted a scholarship from West Point Academy. He chose the military school over twenty other options due to my advocating for this lifestyle for him. However, after a year at West Point, he decided that it was not the right fit for him, and he accepted a scholarship at Tulane University and moved back to Louisiana.

Although Julius's switch to Tulane moved him away from my dream of his becoming an officer in the military, I supported his decision. I had done my job of advocating for him as a child when he was incapable of making decisions for himself; however, he was now a young adult capable of making important life decisions. His respect for my advice meant so much to me. He still comes to me for guidance and advice before he makes his decisions, but at the end of the day, he knows he should do what is best for him.

In 2014 May, Julius earned a Bachelor of Science degree in finance and a minor in entrepreneurship from the A.B. Freeman Business School at Tulane University in New Orleans. However, he was unable to participate in his graduation ceremonies because one week before commencement, he reported as a defensive end to the Houston Texans (NFL) Football Summer Training Camp.

Later he was released to the Seattle Seahawks. Instead of experiencing his college graduation ceremonies, Julius worked his way to the XLIX Super Bowl; and on his behalf, I had the amazing honor of accepting his college diploma along with his academic awards.

Ways To Help ...

Children are impressionable and uncertain of their place in the world. They depend on us to ensure their needs are met. Advocacy is about protection—the "Mama Bear" instinct drives parents to take control of acquiring resources for their children. As children grow older, we transition from **advocate** to **advisor**.

Ways to Help Your Child Grow and Develop into the Person He/She Is Meant to Be

- Teach self-awareness
- Observe the behavior and habits of each child
- Assess the personal needs of each child
- Based on a child's innate skills, begin to plan and prepare for his or her future
- Seek outside resources based on the child's natural abilities
- Always encourage your child to do and be the best
- Always tell your children you believe in them
- Tell them they are smart, beautiful, and capable of greatness
- Understand the difference between a behavior and a personality: compliment an acceptable behavior or correct an unacceptable behavior but respect your child's personality because that is who he or she is
- Daily foster/plan skill development activities for your children
- Know what character traits—such as respectfulness, trustworthiness, honesty, etc.—you want your child to master/learn then day-to-day create scenarios and experiences to teach as well as practice those traits.

Supplemental Resources

- Suggested reading: *Emotional Intelligence* by Daniel Goldman, *The Wait* by Devon Franklin and Meagan Good; "Teach My Learning Kits" www.teachmy.com
- Suggested viewing: *The Lion King*
- Suggested listening: "The Greatest Love of All" by Whitney Houston

Tell Your Story:

A: Advocate And Advisor

*"Give your child lots of great eye contact;
it's the secret to a great relationship."*

—Laura Cooper

Chapter 3
R: RELATIONSHIP/RESPECT

Everyone has heard the **aphorism** *we teach others how to treat us.* When it comes to our children, we teach them not only how to treat us, but how to treat every other person with whom they'll interact throughout their lives. This is why it's essential to develop a wholesome, exemplary **relationship** with our children.

The physical and cognitive growth of children is predicated on how they live their lives, and the relationship between parent and child sets the precedent for future interpersonal contact, from friends and romantic partners, to business colleagues and employers.

By using the model of advocate to advisor, you demonstrate the dynamics of a successful relationship to your child—one including fairness, trust, honesty, support, and reliability. As your relationship grows, you will teach your children to share themselves with others in a meaningful way, and to guard themselves when they feel uncomfortable with how they're being treated.

You are the most important role model in your child's life, so it is imperative, especially when your child is around, to demonstrate successful relationship habits with everyone you interact with. This awareness will not only create an exemplary model for your child, but may also improve many of your own relationships. Your bond with your child is the origin of his/her social proficiency for the rest of his/her life, so create one that is healthy, positive, and framed with open communication.

The relationship counselor Dr. Harville Hendrix developed a theory of "Imago" relationships that underscores how impactful the parent-child dynamic can be throughout life. According to Hendrix, children are born healthy and whole, but they become wounded during childhood as they face hardships, challenges, and disappointments. Through this, the child creates an "Imago," or unconscious blueprint, of the positive and negative traits in their parents.

Later in life, people attempt to heal their childhood wounds by entering a romantic relationship with a person who shares those traits. The relationship allows the child to work through parental issues they developed as a youngster but were unable to fully process until adulthood.

Does that mean our children will end up dating someone like us? Perhaps, but not necessarily; what it does mean is that the relationship we share with our children in their younger years is internalized within them and carried through the rest of their lives, so it's important to make it a good one.

Personal Story
Mindset and Pursuit

I Need Motivation

One morning while getting ready for the school and work day, Titus stated, "Mama, I need motivation." I stopped what I was doing, sat on the floor with him, looked him in the eyes, and said, "Son, what are you motivated to do?" He commenced describing a litany of hoped-for future accomplishments: his hopes and dreams of securing a scholarship and graduating from a Division I college then becoming a professional basketball player in the NBA.

I then asked him, "How do you plan to achieve your goals, and what is your plan of action?" He looked at me speechless. I broke the silence, instructing him to write down what he needed to accomplish his dreams of graduating from college and playing at a professional level. I told him to start where he is right now, at that time a freshman in high school, and create a plan A and a plan B.

Years later, at dinner, Titus said, "Mama, remember the plan of action I laid out?"

I said, "Of course I do."

He continued, "I have accomplished everything on that list," and commenced in highlighting his numerous achievements. (www.beaboutit.com)

Once more, I said, "Son, if you see yourself as a giant," and he finished the sentence, "you will act like one!" We laughed out loud and then both said, "Now what?" He has a new plan of action now, and I have the utmost confidence that he will, again, accomplish everything on his list. (www.warmsleywealth.com)

Remember to make your BED

In 2001, Julius and I settled down in an eclectic but charming neighborhood mixed with renovated older homes, as well as newer, more modern dwellings. It was an excellent location for us. The school bus route was a few blocks away from his future high school, and public transit also was available, which later served as an emergency transportation alternative for us.

However, from 2001 to 2003, Louisiana experienced a period of low rainfall. Once the weather returned to normal, we learned that our beautiful, 60-year-old home had a problem. When it rained, it not only rained outside but inside, too. We managed to resolve a few structural problems, but the repairs needed were beyond our financial capability and my options were limited. The challenge was overwhelming.

Ironically, it seems the rain preferred early morning hours and weekday exhibitions, i.e. school and workdays. For the next few years, every rainy season was an insufferable, painful, and recurring nightmare, especially because of its obnoxious timing, i.e. 2–3 a.m. A 20–gallon water vacuum resolved the inside flooding problem. It worked, but the intermittent task was exhausting.

When this saga started, Julius was around nine. He was helpful and dedicated to the chore at hand, but I was concerned about his ability to switch from his role as man of the house—helping his mom survive a very challenging adult real life situation—to his role as a student and also understanding how to enjoy being a kid.

According to research, the brain does not completely develop until the age of 25. Julius was only nine. Therefore, I crafted a mental acronym for him called BED: **B**e respectful; **E**njoy being a kid; **D**efine your role.

The goal of this mnemonic was for him to learn how to naturally shift his mindset from being the little man of the hour at home and resuming his role as a child at school and also in the community. Whenever I dropped him off at the bus stop or school, I would say, "Julius, remember to make your BED." This strategy worked for him.

My Friend BUD

But when Julius was in the sixth grade, he came home every day with sadness in his eyes. I asked him, "What's wrong?" and with teary eyes he said, "Students at school call me 'Julius Germ.'"

He explained how those words made him feel, and I asked him, "How do you feel when you receive a compliment from your teacher or friends?"

Tears were rolling down his face, but he smiled and said, "I feel great!"

I shared wisdom with him that my mother shared with me: If you can't say something nice, don't say anything at all; treat people how you want to be treated; compliment someone when you see them doing something nice; acknowledge one's triumph for the day; open a door for someone; pick up a dropped item; be polite; be kind.

I asked, "How do you think you will feel when people do these things to you? How do you feel when you do these things for others?"

Again, flashing that big beautiful smile, he said, "Great!"

I said, "Okay. So, that is what I want you to focus on—understanding what triggers feelings of happiness and sadness. The goal is to remove the negative from your mind and replace it with positives. Whenever students call you 'Julius Germ,' give out five compliments to five different people, and the joy you will get from doing good will make you feel better!"

To help him remember the importance of understanding these things, I created the acronym BUD. **B**e respectful, **U**nderstand yourself, and **D**efine your role. Every day when I would drop him off at school, I would say, "Julius, remember to compliment your new friend BUD."

At the age of nine years old, Julius entered a "What was the best advice your parents gave you contest?" The contest was sponsored by a local Sporting Goods store. He answered the questionnaire explaining the **BED** acronym. He won! The prize was a pair of sneakers. He decided to replace my worn out sneakers for a brand new pair.

From nine to fourteen years old, *"the acronyms"*, **BED** and **BUD**, played major roles in Julius' mental framework, as well as his social and physical development. The mental messages helped him stay focused, build self-respect; develop a sense of confidence and self-worth while perfecting his athletic and leadership skills. As a family, individually and separately, we engaged in extracurricular activities such as working the concession stand at his games and serving holiday meals at shelters but above all we developed an unrestricted parent-child line of communication.

Throughout Julius tenure under my care, he enjoyed the personalized mental messages transitioning smoothly from school age to adolescent stages of development. However, the *"adolescent stage"* was a turning point because it is the last stage before adulthood and also a time where he really needed my parental guidance as well as the friendship of other adults.

At this stage, decision making, thinking about his future in the workplace as well as other major benchmarks began to form. I knew high school would be filled with new directions such as social relationship building and staying on track regarding college preparation. Therefore, continuing his mental development in high school, I, appropriately, returned to using BED. Instead of **B**e Respectful; **E**njoy being a kid; **D**efine your **R**ole, this time the BED acronym meant **B**e Respectful; **E**njoy your life; **D**efine your **R**ole.

From elementary to middle to high school, the customized mentalities played a crucial role in developing my sons' mindsets. Today, the messages remain part of our e-message transactions. Now, they respond with an image of a fist bump and LOL.

After all these years, when I receive their text messages instead of physically witnessing big beautiful smiles and hugs, the visual of those physical images remain steadfast in my consciousness. The mindsets we manifested worked not only for them, they worked for me as well.

Ways to Build...

Your bond with your children is the origin of their social proficiency for the rest of their lives, so create bonds that are healthy, positive, and framed with open, conscious communication. Teach your children the dynamics of mutually beneficial relationships—fairness, trust, honesty, support, and reliability.

Ways to Build and Understand Relationships

- Schedule weekly family meetings
- Involve your child in the decision making process as early as possible
- Allow each child time to speak up at every meeting
- Talk to your child about your family life, childhood, and personality
- Teach your child how to understand the meaning and importance of "self-knowledge"
- Teach your child the relationship chain: God, family, helping others
- Show your child how to deal with people, first with family members
- Demonstrate and teach the pillars of character: respectfulness, honesty, trustworthiness, citizenship, caring, fairness
- Emphasize the importance of good eye contact and also practice the skill

Supplemental Resources

- Suggested reading: *The Nudge* by Richard H. Thalen and Cass R. Sunstien
- Suggested viewing: *War Room*
- Suggested listening: "He saw the Best in Me" by Marvin Sapp

Tell Your Story:

_____

_____

_____

_____

_____

_____

_____

_____

_____

_____

_____

_____

_____

_____

_____

_____

_____

_____

R: Relationship/Respect

> *"Tell me and I forget;*
> *teach me and I may remember;*
> *involve me and I learn."*
>
> —Benjamin Franklin

Chapter 4

E: EXPERIENCE

At its core, life is the summation of our individual **experiences**. Each moment is a building block that will eventually surface in our character and express itself in some facet of our personality. The hefty impact of our experiences is obvious throughout life, but it's especially important during childhood, when each experience carries an exponentially large weight that can effect development in countless ways.

For this reason, parents must be cognizant at all times of the experiences they offer their children. As parents, we feel the responsibility of balancing calm, peaceful normalcy with exciting, unique occurrences that can awaken in our children a zest for life that ensures they will experience their existence to the fullest. One of the most important examples you will set for your child is your reaction to and handling of tragic experiences.

Whether it is the death of a loved one or a debilitating accident, teaching your child how to process and deal with tragedy in a healthy way is critical. These experiences, although unfortunate, will prepare your child for unpredictable occurrences in life, and they will teach him/her how to continue to live in the midst of heartbreak.

It's important for children to partake in a wide array of experiences for several reasons. Abraham Maslow's hierarchy of needs theory states that in order to advance to the next step, children must completely master each need. For example, if a child is attempting to become self-actualized but never mastered the belonging stage, he/she will continue to regress to the belonging stage until mastering it.

The only way to ensure mastery of these needs is to provide a variety of experiences which expose our children to new things so that they may develop a personal worldview. By introducing our children to new, invigorating, healthy experiences, we can, in effect, give them the tools to create more exciting lives for themselves.

Journalist Joshua Foer, in his book *Moonwalking with Einstein*, discovered that "monotony collapses time; novelty unfolds it." We are all familiar with the feeling of "day-in, day-out." When your life is repetitive and lacking excitement and change, you tend to lose all sense of time.

By experiencing new adventures, both big and small, our lives begin to feel much more complete and accomplished. If we instill this desire for adventure and discovery in our children at a young age, it will lead to more fulfilled and satisfying lives for them.

Personal Story
Walk Into a Room Like You Own It . . .

As a child, I remember sharing the excitement with my friends during the weeks leading up to Halloween. We all dressed up as our favorite characters ranging from movie stars to news reporters to musicians. On Halloween night, we waited eagerly for darkness to fall and for the streetlights to flicker on, signaling it was time to trick-or-treat.

Halloween may be interpreted as a "spooky" night, but as children, we weren't afraid. Our neighborhood was safe. Caring adults were with us the whole night to guide us from door to door and we were received with warmth at every household.

We would approach each home, and when the door opened, we'd earnestly yell, "Trick or Treat!" But our neighbors always gave us treats, so we never even considered tricking them, nor did we ever consider the possibility of tricking each other. Halloween was a night of treats!

The anticipation for the night kept us in check behaviorally, and we all knew that if we misbehaved, we would not be allowed to take part in the festivities. Furthermore, if we were disrespectful to anyone during the night—child or adult—we would be sent straight home.

Back in our homes by 9 p.m., our curfew, we carefully counted and sorted the treats we collected, so we could boast about our haul to our friends the next day at school (often wearing residual makeup from our costumes the night before).

Today, Halloween is much different, and "When times change, so must we," (President Obama, 2014). In the mid-'90s, local and national newspapers were filled with articles of adults being arrested after contaminating candy with cyanide, pins, and needles and distributing them to children on Halloween night.

These changing times have forced us, especially as parents, to be suspicious and hyper-vigilant about the people with whom our children interact, particularly those we do not know personally. In the midst of these terrible changes, one thing has remained constant: parenting.

Julius was a young boy during this turbulent and newly suspicious time. He loved Halloween. It was the one time of year I allowed him to abundantly indulge in sweets. His Halloween experience differed greatly from my own, and because of my concern, I decided to change the direction of Halloween for him.

When he was six, local churches began to hold Halloween parties where the children dressed in their costumes and went trick-or-treating inside the recreation room of the church. It sounded like a perfect, safe environment for me to take Julius to celebrate Halloween.

Anticipation was high in the days leading up to Halloween night, but it finally arrived! We pulled up to the church and parked about 25 feet from the entrance. We sat in the car for a moment so Julius could adjust his costume, and I looked into his beautiful brown eyes and said, "Son, you know you will be the only little boy of color there tonight? How do you feel about that?"

He looked at me with an air of confidence and a big beautiful smile and innocently said, "Mama, all I want is to get lots of candy and have a great time. Nothing else matters."

I smiled and said, "You see that entrance? I want you to open the door for me then I will walk in front of you. I want you to walk into the room like you own it. Nobody will know the difference."

On October 31, 1996, the transformation of the celebration of Halloween made me realize the change in my parenting mindset. My concerns caused me to alter tradition and "normal" plans for my son and me in order to ensure his health, safety, and happiness. Through this experience, I was able to observe and assess my son's growth and mental development.

For the next eleven years, we continued participating in organized Halloween festivities, but in middle school, we returned to the traditional, neighborhood door-to-door activities. When Halloween rolled around that year, we set out to have fun and bonding time.

But Julius was in his sophomore year of high school. He was 6-feet tall, 185 lbs. and a popular athlete. He was cheerfully focused on the good times of past Halloween night experiences, but 15 minutes into knocking on doors with other kids and moms standing nearby, Julius encountered a neighbor who refused to give him treats because he said Julius was too old. Julius was crushed, and he quickly reflected on the sadder *Julius germ* experience (see Chapter 3, Relationship's Personal Story: Pursuit and Mindset).

After discussing how we resolved similar episodes—*"be respectful; be fair; be kind"* approach—we continued knocking on doors, which proved to be a beneficial decision. Shortly thereafter, we called it a night. On the walk home, we shared family stories.

As we approached the carport, renewed and flashing that big beautiful smile and sharing a hug with me, Julius said, "Thanks Ma. We had another great time together."

I told him, "Son, the honor was all mine."

The following year, Julius befriended a first-grader son of a friend. He invited Julius to trick-or-treat in his neighborhood, and Julius accepted. This time, Julius was in charge of a small Krewe of Munchkins, and once again, moms in tow trailed slightly behind them. That Halloween night, I witnessed a maturing teenager, an extraordinary gift to society, and the silhouette of a good parent.

However, unknowingly, that unforgettable Halloween experience was our last one together. In Julius' senior year, Halloween was on a Friday—high school football game night. Instead of the usual trick-or-treating experience, we opted to share burgers, fries, and memories of Halloweens past.

And yes, they won the football game. College coaches were in attendance, witnessing Julius as one of the star players of the game, assessing his exceptional talent and contemplating scholarship offers. That Halloween night was the best I ever experienced. As for me, I was fulfilled!

Ways To Expose . . .

By now, we know that we learn best by actually doing things rather than simply hearing of other's trials and errors. Do not be afraid to let your children make mistakes. While books, movies, and songs are supplemental resources, exposing them to new situations and experiences will truly enhance their development. Have faith in your child's decision-making abilities as well as in yourself as a parent and role model.

Ways to Expose Your Children to Various Experiences and Define Their Unique Abilities

- Discuss roles children play in the family unit
- Here are a few examples of novel experiences:
  Have a picnic in the backyard
  Experience New York's New Year's Eve celebration in front the television dressed in formal attire and drinking sparkling water
  Visit your state parks, attend local and regional festivals
  Visit observatories
  Explore your state or travel where your resources can take the family
- Create family rituals like game night
- Focus on creating your family's legacies and making memories
- Spend time together as a family and also dedicate personal time with each child and your spouse or partner

Supplemental Resources

- Suggested reading: *The Marshmallow Test* by Dr. Walter Mischel
- Suggested viewing: *Pursuit of Happyness*
- Suggested listening: "Good Morning" by Mandisa and "Happy" by Pharrell

Tell Your Story:

_____

_____

_____

_____

_____

_____

_____

_____

_____

_____

_____

_____

_____

_____

_____

_____

_____

_____

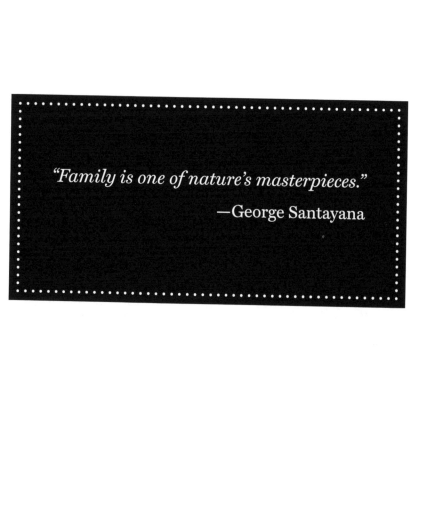

"Family is one of nature's masterpieces."

—George Santayana

Chapter 5

N: NATURAL / NURTURING

espite its challenges and hardships, parenting is a natural skill that is innate to all of us. We all have the skills to do the job and do it well, but we must learn to tap into that natural ability in order to reach our full potential as caregivers.

Nearly every parent has experienced this problem: it's 3 a.m. and we're awakened by the cries of our baby. We get out of bed, assess our child's needs, and feed him. We get the baby back to sleep and settle back under our own covers. Then, an hour later, the baby is crying again. What does he need?

It's up to parents to use our natural instincts to connect with the child and discern what else is making him unhappy. Situations like this are often baffling, but the first step to solving the puzzle is realizing that we're wired with the ability to do it right.

Evolutionary biology says an organism is only truly successful once it has produced viable offspring. It's about survival of the fittest—the ones who are strong enough to create descendants to carry on the species have served their big-picture purpose. Of course, that's only a narrow view of the importance of being a parent, but it nonetheless speaks to the fact that it's genetic to be a successful parent.

All the answers are within the special connection we share with our children. The natural bond between parent and child is sacred. It's at once biological, emotional, and spiritual. No relationship we experience can match the depth of that bond. So when you're trying to figure out the right way to handle a parenting dilemma, trust your instincts.

Listen to that special frequency deep inside yourself that keeps you in alignment with your child's needs. We all have the answers and the abilities—the key is realizing that we have them and learning to trust them.

Personal Story
Creative and Endless Parenting

Work Hard: I Know I Can; Be What I Want to Be

At thirteen years old, my son—who at the time was 5'4" and 110 lbs.—dreamed of becoming a professional basketball player. Titus was naturally quick and excelled as a young point guard. However, he knew that most professional point guards were a minimum of six feet tall, and he was uncertain he would ever reach such a height.

He loved basketball. He breathed, ate, and dreamed basketball. Day in and day out, it was always on his mind; however, his soul was troubled and heartbroken as he digested comments about his small stature interfering with his success as a player. These conversations eventually negatively impacted his thoughts about playing at the next level.

One day, he was walking underneath the ceiling fan, and I screamed, "Titus, duck!" Naturally, he was startled, but he trusted my command, dropped his backpack, and dropped to the ground, perched like a tiger ready to pounce. He turned and looked directly into my eyes and said, "Mother, what it is?"

I said, "Son, if you see yourself as a giant, you will act like one."

He looked stunned. I watched as his confusion transformed into joy and confidence. He gave me a bear hug and smiling at me brightly, he said, "Thanks, Mom. I got it!"

Eventually, Titus grew to 5'11" and 190 lbs. After graduating high school, he was offered numerous scholarships from top universities around the country. In 1995 he was a McDonald's All-American, and he was also listed in USA Today's top 125 athletes. He went on to play Division I college basketball, and after earning a Bachelor of Arts degree in communications, he went on to play with the Boston Celtics. He ended his professional basketball career in Europe with awards for Rookie and Athlete of the Year.

When he returned to Louisiana, he was offered a role in the movie *Glory Road*—portraying one of his basketball heroes, Jo Jo White, who played for the University of Kansas Men's Basketball team, represented the U.S. in the 1968 Summer Olympics, and played professional basketball for the Boston Celtics.

Throughout his career, he never forgot the mental message of "*See yourself as a giant.*" This message kept him grounded and focused on success and ensured his faith in his own abilities. In his book, *Don't Talk About It, Be About It,* Titus recounts this message and others like it, documenting examples of my support of his abilities, hopes, and dreams.

From his childhood, I positioned him for future opportunities while nurturing his natural abilities in all areas, guiding him to the path on which I believed he would find success and happiness. He achieved both success and happiness, and that's a win for both of us!

Nip It in the Bud

Today, elementary and secondary schools as well as institutions of higher learning subscribe to Learning Management Systems (LMS). This system documents classroom attendance and participation, monitors quiz and exam scores, and tracks homework assignments. LMS has been proven to strengthen the teacher-student relationship as well as actually improve the academic success of the students. Additionally, when necessary, the system has the capability to create a virtual classroom, for example with a home-bound student.

From a parent's perspective, this online education program is an extension of the classroom because parents can monitor their child's classroom and academic performance. I found it useful when Julius was in elementary and high school.

Throughout Julius's elementary and middle years, he was actively involved in sports and he managed to successfully balance school work with his extracurricular activities. We incorporated in our family meetings the online academic assessment discussion in real time. However, in Julius's freshman year in high school, the system proved its worth. High school sports were of a more serious nature. He participated in four sports and he was never out of a sport season, i.e. from football to basketball to track to weight lifting to ballet.

However, at one of our family meetings, I learned through LMS that he missed an English assignment and his scores did not reflect his academic potential. We discussed this matter and I informed him that I would visit his school the next day. I spoke with his English teacher regarding his classroom attitude, manners, and academic performance. After the meeting and before I left school that day, I informed Julius that he will miss practice for the rest of the week. He did not argue with me but he had to face his coach with my decision.

After he informed his football coach of my academic punishment, I received a call from his coach. "Ms. Warmsley," he sternly started off the conversation, I totally understand your concern of Julius missing his assignments and not reaching his fullest academic potential but to miss practice is not good for the team. I will respect your decision but next time Julius misses his work, please allow me to punish him." I agreed and he thanked me for staying on top of his academics. Julius never missed another assignment and he finished his high school years on the honor roll.

Trilogy of Life

Throughout their growing years and beyond, our children will experience the three Ts: transition, turmoil, and transformation. The trilogy. It's my version of the Trilogy of Life. When Titus was very young, I divorced his dad. Therefore, as a young child, he did not experience a traditional father-son relationship. However, one day, I noticed a mannerism in my pre-teen child that reminded me of his dad.

I said, "WOW, how did that happen?" Then I realized that children naturally inherit traits of their parents—it's genetic. Lesson learned. Therefore, my parenting strategy was to focus on the difference between accepting a personality and correcting a behavior.

Part I: Transition (Birth to . . .)

"We have different gifts, according to the grace given to each of us. If your gift is prophesying, then prophesy in accordance with your faith." Romans 12:6. During the transition stage, parents have total control over their children's development.

Children experience the **transition** period under your administration. Parents, prepare your children for their tomorrows by laying down a basic foundation, and helping them develop a strong moral compass. *"How to Raise Good Parents"* is a model parenting guide for you to consider. Teach them self-regulation and self-respect but also notice personality and behavior changes.

At 10, Titus naturally discovered his abilities and mental aptitude. He was in constant prayer and strove always to do the right thing. He was focused, loyal to me, committed to his siblings, and dedicated to being the best. He was fully determined not to leave his development to chance or his achievement to luck. He easily transitioned from one stage to another. Not all children transition easily, however. Your role as a parent is to naturally nurture your child's gifts but first understand his disposition and continuously observe how he perceives his world.

Part II: Turmoil (10 to . . .)

"Make a tree good and its fruit will be good, make a tree bad and its fruit will be bad, for the tree is recognized by his fruit." Matthew 12:33. For some children, this stage I have named "turmoil" may not be turbulent at all. As a parent, you know your child by now. However, some children may need more attention and patience than others. This stage was a difficult period for Marcus. My goal for him was to identify his strengths and weaknesses and help him understand consequences of his actions.

Parenting is work and you have to work hard at it. In my parenting approach, I customized my parenting strategy (*see Chapter 3, Personal Story: I Need Motivation*) to fit each child's needs.

Part III: Transformation (18 to . . .)

"Do not conform to this world, but be transformed by the renewal of your mind, that by testing you may discern what is the will of God, what is good and acceptable and perfect." Roman 12:2

As a parent, begin the preparation of your child's journey early through moral and mental development. Create developmental messages based on each child's personality. To optimize the development of your child and yourself, remain close to your spiritual roots.

The basis of your child's journey starts with Proverbs 22:6: "Train up a child the way he should go; when he is older he will not depart from his teaches". If your child strays from your teaching, he will walk it back because this is all he knows.

Throughout life, we all will travel through these stages of development. The Trilogy is systematic, and each stage may yield positive or negative results—it depends on the child, the environment, the resources, etc. but more importantly the mindset of the parent(s) or caregiver(s).

As the child moves closer to his adult and parenting journey, the outcome of each sequence depends on how well Part I Trilogy was implemented and later mastered. (*See Chapter 2: Advocate and Advisor: Maslow's Hierarchy chart*).

Where Are They (We) Now?

We celebrate special events together. We share— weekly quotes, movies to see, books of the month, and motivational songs. While continuing our family rituals and traditions, my sons are also writing their own stories and creating their own legacies. They are transitioning into their adult and family-hood roles.

They are beginning to experience *"The Walk"* (as in: "in my shoes") and *"The Talk"* (adult-to-adult conversations with me). Now, they know what it means to be a friend with an adult parent—one who is trustworthy, responsible, and accountable for her actions.

Time is always on our minds—deadlines, goals, countdowns to vacation, holidays etc. Time is the most precious of all our possessions—more than any material things or amount of money—and it is important to remember to teach your child just this.

Ways to Develop . . .

In the midst of chaos and turmoil, rely on your instincts to make decisions. You know yourself and your child better than anyone else, and you have the power and capability of making the best decisions possible for your family. You know what works for you and your family, and this might be different from others' practices; however, you should always trust your instincts as a parent.

Ways to Develop Common Practices as Well as Creative and Strategic Parenting Skills

- Trust yourself first, and follow your instincts
- Know your child: observe behaviors and evaluate personalities
- Talk to your child about your assessment of his/her skills, i.e., what he/she likes or dislikes
- Genetics matters: Talk to your child about how much she mirrors the behavior of dad or mom or other family members
- Foster the importance of understanding family background
- Teach your children the importance of gut feelings and trusting intuition
- Create an environment of happiness in the home by showing your children how to love life
- Show your children how to be responsible and accountable for their behavior
- Show them how to live *today*, be thankful for *yesterday*, be grateful for *tomorrow* [Titus Warmsley].

Supplemental Resources

- Suggested reading: *David and Goliath* by Malcolm Gladwell
- Suggested viewing: *The Great Debaters* with Denzel Washington
- Suggested listening: "Eye of the Tiger" by Survivor and "Mama" by Boyz to Men

Tell Your Story:

N: Natural / Nurturing

_____

_____

_____

> "Spending *TIME* with your children
> is more important than
> spending *MONEY* on children."
>
> —Anthony Douglas Williams

Illustration by Ricky J. Nicholas

Chapter 6

T: TIME

It took two years for the French to build the Eiffel Tower, four years for Michelangelo to paint the Sistine Ceiling, and more than 2,000 years to construct the entire Great Wall of China. Anything worth doing takes time, and that's certainly the case with parenting.

Having a child is a lifetime commitment, and it starts even before you hear the first cry from your new baby's lungs. The nine months you spend waiting on that bundle of joy aren't just meant for picking names and catering to the cravings of pregnancy. The gestation period is a meaningful time when parents begin "nesting," or preparing for their child's arrival. This means taking the time to properly develop a family plan and establish the environment in which your child will be introduced to the world.

It's important to plan far in advance and also think about how your parents' parenting styles will impact yours. Think ahead and answer important questions that could shape your child's upbringing. How will you monitor his diet? How much time will he spend playing outdoors versus watching television? When should you introduce children to technology? How will you evaluate your child's friends to know if they're trustworthy? How will you talk to him or her about sex? Deciding these things early makes your path smoother in the future.

As a conscious parent, it's not only about the amount of time you spend evaluating your parenting style. It is also about making the most of each moment you spend with your children. The time you spend with each child is what is important, and spending quality time should be reflected in your family's lifestyle. We might spend two hours sitting next to our children as they surf the Internet, but what have we gained in that time?

Are those two hours more valuable than 30 minutes spent reading together? Or 15 minutes praying as a family? Meaningful engagement with a parent is just as important to children as healthy food, clean clothes, and a warm bed. Without it, they're missing part of what they need to become the best version of themselves.

Personal Story
Parenting Is a Lifestyle

When I think back on my childhood, my fondest memories are those of summers with my relatives—visiting Grandpa D's sugar cane farm, traveling to Houston for our annual family vacation to visit with Aunt Gert and her family, peering over the counter watching Mama (maternal grandmother) make homemade cake and ice cream for our Sunday gatherings, or canning fruits and vegetables with Nanny and Aunt Dorothy.

Being together as a family was imperative for us. Although I may not have realized it then, it was during these times that I learned what kind of parent I wanted to be. My parents modeled good parenting and also taught me what it meant to be part of a family. I continued their legacy of family traditions with my own children.

All three of my sons experienced their first hair cut at age two, and afterwards, every other Saturday became breakfast date and barber shop day. Birthday celebrations were always spent together—at home, or at school, or the park, depending on the day—and we held family meetings every Sunday to discuss the various activities and events of the upcoming week. Those meetings were also for talking about my parenting strategy, personal goals, successes and failures, etc.

As my children grew older and began to create their own, more specialized lives, our family time changed. Face-to-face meetings became phone calls since we all lived in different parts of the country. Our conversations became more individually focused and driven because each child was on a completely different path.

While we will always be a family unit, I realized the importance of focusing on each child individually in order to best nourish his strengths and abilities. I encouraged them to make individual decisions which began to take precedence over collective decisions, and it was during this transitory period that I would morph from advocate to advisor for each of my sons, as needed.

Our rituals changed as my boys grew up, but we have always made an effort to come together whether for a weekend or a five-minute conversation on the phone. No matter how hectic our lives are, we always make time for each other, and I made sure each of my children understands the importance of spending time with family.

Ways to Establish ...

At the end of each day, remember to be thankful for the time you have with your child. Our children learn the most from us, as parents, so it is important to show them how to appreciate time spent with family, friends, and loved ones, as well as time spent alone.

Ways to Establish Basic Routines and Teach Habit-Forming Skills–Take the Time To

- Model good behavior for your children. Show them how to do things rather than simply telling them.
- Keep up with societal trends (social media, music, etc.) and understand that each child grows on his or her own schedule.
- Teach by example: proper nutritional and health practices, including exercise (do it together).
- Teach your child the importance of *"me"* time
- Remember that the way you value your *time* with your children should be reflected in your family's lifestyle.

Supplemental Resources

- Suggested reading: *Don't Talk About It ... Be About It!* by Titus Warmsley
- Suggested viewing: *Lincoln* with Daniel Day Lewis
- Suggested listening: "I Am Not Alone" by Kari Jobe

Tell Your Story:

_____

_____

_____

_____

_____

_____

_____

_____

_____

_____

_____

_____

_____

_____

_____

_____

_____

_____

T: Time

95

"*Each day of our lives we make deposits in the memory banks of our children.*"

—Charles R. Swindoll

Chapter 7

I: INVESTMENT

Nothing is free in life except the air we breathe and the grey hairs our children give us. It may not cost us anything to conceive a child, but we spend the rest of our lives hemorrhaging cash to ensure our children have everything they need. It's quite an investment.

The U.S. Department of Agriculture says that a child born to a middle-class family in 2010 will cost its parents $226,920 over the first 18 years of life—that's $286,860 when adjusted for inflation. Food, shelter, education, health care, and other necessities aren't cheap, and they're not costs we want to skimp on, either.

Parenting is an unpaid job that requires a second job to pay for it. Of course, the investment is more than worth it. Parents are rewarded by seeing their children happy and achieving their goals. Love is bonus, not payback. But the cost of having kids can't be ignored, and that's why it's important never to lose sight of the endless expenses that come with being a mother or father.

Children are investments in themselves. As parents, our goal is to help them create the most human capital as possible in the time spent under our roofs. We do this by advising, guiding, and challenging our children to help them realize their full potential. We want to give our children the best parts of ourselves so that these parts of us will live on in them and continue to be passed down through their offspring as well.

As the media theorist and cultural critic Neil Postman wrote, "Children are the living messages we send to a time we cannot see." Long after we're gone, our children will carry

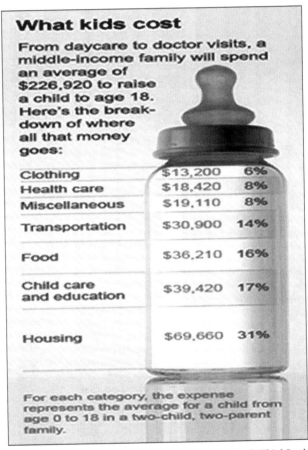

What kids cost

From daycare to doctor visits, a middle-income family will spend an average of $226,920 to raise a child to age 18. Here's the breakdown of where all that money goes:

Clothing	$13,200	6%
Health care	$18,420	8%
Miscellaneous	$19,110	8%
Transportation	$30,900	14%
Food	$36,210	16%
Child care and education	$39,420	17%
Housing	$69,660	31%

For each category, the expense represents the average for a child from age 0 to 18 in a two-child, two-parent family.

Source: U.S. Department of Agriculture. Photo: BananaStock/ThinkStock.

our legacy, our memory, and our DNA into a future we will never be a part of. Our children perpetuate our family name and family values long after we are no longer around to shape those things ourselves. The children you raise reflect on you forever, so it's important to make your investment in them a good one.

Personal Story
Children Are Gifts to Society

Education Is Not Optional

Children are investments. As parents, we should view our children as future contributors to society. It is of the utmost importance to prepare our children for their future roles by investing in both their economic and social capitals.

Harvey MacKay wrote, in his book *To Get Ahead, Use Your Head*: "Knowing how to analyze a situation and how to execute an action plan will put you ahead of the game in the long run. There's nothing wrong with having a leg up on your competition—it's how you win. The combination of hard work and smart work is the formula for success.

"Think about what needs to be done, and then think again about the best way to accomplish it—not necessarily the way you've always done it, or the fastest way, and certainly not the hardest way. Never make work harder than it has to be. That's just a colossal waste of time." These are lessons I tried to instill in my sons.

The first major investment I taught my children about was education. As soon as they could understand what I meant, I began telling them, "Education is not optional. It is mandatory. It's an investment." When they were in middle school, I began preparing them for college.

I assured them I would finance their secondary education; however, they were responsible for paying for their college educations. Their mission and responsibility was to secure a scholarship—either athletic or academic—to complete their undergraduate degrees without an educational mortgage over their heads.

In order to assist and guide them to obtain this goal, I taught them the importance of working *smart* versus simply working *hard.* MacKay illustrates this concept in a story of two lumberjacks:

"Both were strong and determined, hoping to win the prize. But one was hardworking and ambitious, chopping down every tree in his path at the fastest pace possible, while the other appeared to be a little more laid-back, methodically chopping trees and pacing himself. The go-getter worked all day, skipping his lunch break, expecting that his superior effort would be rewarded.

His opponent, however, took an hour-long lunch and then resumed his steady pace. In the end, the eager beaver was dismayed to lose to his 'lazier' competition. Thinking he deserved to win after his hard work, he finally approached his opponent and said, 'I just don't understand. I worked longer and harder than you, and went hungry to get ahead. You took a break, and yet you still won. It just doesn't seem fair. Where did I go wrong?' The winner responded, 'While I was taking my lunch break, I was sharpening my ax.'"

Working smart with your children and teaching them to work smart on their own is no easy task. First, spend time with them. Carefully assess their strengths and weaknesses. Help to steer them towards their talents and nurse specific interests.

Titus dreamed of playing basketball as a boy, but he was also interested in football and track. I discouraged him from playing all three sports, and I asked him to choose one to focus on. However, after consulting with others about Titus's basketball career, I learned that the three sports complemented each other, and the cross training would assist his pursuit of a serious career in basketball.

Through this experience, I realized that sometimes I'd make a mistake, but that help is out there. I learned to seek counseling and ask for help when in doubt. Although I was a single mother, I was not alone in raising my three sons. Working with my boys and trusted others, I created a set of guidelines and established a committee of advisors to assist us in our journey. Once I obtained the necessary knowledge, the honors and tributes followed.

The most valuable strategy through this journey was to develop an action plan and to implement it, with the goals and benefits of education always at the forefront. I carefully created a family mission, or philosophy, and I modified it as time passed. Goals were achieved, and new ones were created.

MacKay articulates my philosophy: "Successful people have a clear vision of where they are headed and also a plan of action. The application of the 'work hard, but work smart' lesson applies to children as well. Today, even more so, parents need to not tell their children what to do but how to do it, then find the pathway to help them journey down the road to success."

Education Is an Investment

My parents' goals for their children were for us to speak good English, get a good education, and get a good job. These goals were deeply embedded in the minds of my parents, especially my mom. She knew firsthand the difficulties faced by people without language proficiency.

In her early years of school, she and her older siblings were not proficient in English. Their parents spoke Creole, and at that time, people of Louisiana did not embrace those who spoke English poorly. So, her education experience was not a pleasant one. She decided to quit school later on, vowing that when she became a parent, her children would not be embarrassed and would complete their educations differently, starting with mastery of the language.

My mother didn't want us to learn her language. At the time, she did not see the benefits of teaching her culture to us because she was made to feel ashamed of her background. Although she perfected the art of parenting by focusing on the benefits of family values, she did not follow through with teaching her children the value of her rich culture. I am sorry about that, and encourage all parents to imbue their children with an understanding of what came before, and encourage respectfulness towards it. This is possible while parents are empowered to practice parenting positivity—focusing on the good, not the bad. Include in the family strategic plan the benefits of learning a new language as well as embracing your culture. As a result your children will grow proud of who they are.

All she wanted for us was to do better and be better than she. Her mission was accomplished when we graduated from high school, but she did not realize how much of an asset it would have been for her children nowadays if we spoke a second language.

Because of her lack of education, the only job she secured was house cleaning, but it did not stop her from dreaming of bettering herself and her family. She worked for a reporter, politicians, doctors, lawyers, and business owners. She witnessed first-hand what education could do for people and their families. She also acquired excellent marketplace skills, but the lack of an education held her back.

She desired a better job for herself and wanted the best for her children. My dad was a master tradesman. His job provided benefits, allowing us to live well, but she dreamed of moving up from working in homes to working in offices or a hospital.

In the late 80s, her dream was to secure a position with Pinecrest Developmental Center in Pineville, Louisiana. Although she missed being hired at Pinecrest, she reached her dream of working in and later retiring from a hospital at St. Francis Cabrini in Alexandria, Louisiana. Not only did she reach that goal, but she took pride in being elected Employee of the Year by her supervisors and peers.

I have accomplished every dream my mom had for me. She instilled in me—through role modeling, love, and determination—that you can be whatever you want to be, but first and foremost, she professed, you must focus on your education and "work hard but smart" at becoming an expert in your field. Her investment in my siblings and me mirrored her dreams for herself. As a result, I dedicated myself to my children's growth and development—just as my parents did for us.

From the conference rooms and offices where I consult to the classrooms and auditoriums where I speak and teach, I try to leave each room tidier than I found it. I know when I leave, someone like my mom comes behind me to clean up.

My mom felt that she did not have any career choice, but she made sure that I did. That's what parents do. They sacrifice. Your children will be your legacy. Your job, as a parent, is to help them define their stories through your lens and also help them understand that in their personal journeys there will be pitfalls in the process.

My parents' modeled empathy and humility and I duplicated their behaviors. I learned from my parents to think beyond today to better prepare my children for tomorrow. I learned from my parents to follow my heart and develop my mind.

The heartbeat of *How to Raise Good Parents* is this: "All parents are born; good parents are developed." Although

I modified my parenting strategy to meet today's parenting needs, I kept my mom's basic common parenting practices: God, family, then helping others.

After all, children are investments! It's been said, "The fruit does not fall too far from the tree." I am my mom's contribution to society—educated and employed, contributor and author, and above all proficient in English. I thank God and I thank my parents for giving me the opportunity to be who I am today.

Like my mom, I dreamed, strategized, and visualized a parenting concept: *How to Raise Good Parents*, and in the process I learned that "children are gifts to society. What's your contribution?"

Ways to Teach . . .

Everything costs money, so it is of the utmost importance to both plan for the financial security of our children as well as teach them how to become financially independent and successful.

Ways to Teach Personal Development/Self-Mastery and How to Position Your Children's Future

- Promote the importance of education from day one
- Promote learning a second language
- Set high expectations—plan and prepare your children to seek and explore opportunities
- Teach your child the basic fundamentals of managing money, i.e. save, share, invest, spend
- Teach your child the importance of planning for the future by being responsible today
- Be an involved parent at home, at school, at church, in the community, etc.
- Explain the difference between personal and professional behaviors then practice the skill set
- Foster connections among family, community, education, religion, as well as other conjoint institutions such as the economy, media, and government

---

Supplemental Resources

- Suggested reading: *Excellent Sheep* by William Deresiewicz, *In Defense of Liberal Education* by Fareed Zaharia, and *Smart is the New Rich* by Christine Romans; TED Talk Guide to Public Speaking by Chris Anderson
- Suggested viewing: *Remember the Titans* with Denzel Washington
- Suggested listening: "You Can Let Go" by Crystal Shawanda and "I Know I Can" by Nas

Tell Your Story:

_____

_____

_____

_____

_____

_____

_____

_____

_____

_____

_____

_____

_____

_____

_____

_____

I: Investment

> *"At the end of the day, the most overwhelming key to a child's success is the positive involvement of parents."*
>
> —Jane D. Hull

Chapter 8

N: NAVIGATION

The world our parents lived in was drastically different from the one we experience, and the same is true for our children. Although society has changed more dramatically in the last 100 years than in any other era, our basic roles and responsibilities as parents have not. Part of what we must do as parents is teach children how to navigate the unknown waters of an ever-changing culture. That's a big job.

Think of all the things our children have today that we never could have dreamed of as children ourselves—iPods, iPads, smartphones, GPS systems, and the list goes on. If we couldn't have anticipated these gadgets a little more than 10 years ago, just imagine what our children may have access to by the time they become adults.

We cannot predict what the world will look like when our children take control of their lives. Therefore, we must not always tell our children what to do, but teach them critical thinking processes that help them distinguish good decisions from bad ones as well as trigger creativity.

External forces such as those I just mentioned often do not align with our parenting plan and may undermine today's parents. In the past, the notions of family and community were greatly supported; however, in today's society, it is much more difficult to control what our children are exposed to.

Many of these outside forces may work in opposition to an individual's parenting values, so it is imperative to teach children early on to nurture positive influences and resist negative influences and distractions that may cause them to veer from the path we lay for them.

Parenting in the 21st Century is about instilling in children the ability to steer their own ship when the need arises. You can teach your children the navigational skills they need to get through life independently in this modern world.

We as parents can—and should—only carry our sons and daughters so far. Eventually they must learn to lead on their own, and we can teach them how by providing an example for them during childhood.

Personal Story
What's Your Contribution?

When my two eldest sons, Marcus and Titus, were pre-teens, I made it a priority to teach them the difference between "Mama's Rules" and "Society's Rules"—the law. Before a day of fun and exploring in New Orleans at the Audubon Zoo, I took them to the local courthouse to teach them an important lesson.

Our chatting and merriment ceased as a line of prisoners in orange jumpsuits filed out the back door of the prison. My boys watched through teary eyes as the prisoners walked rhythmically in unison, chained at the feet, waist, and hands. After observing their reactions to the prisoners, I asked them to step out of the car and hold out their hands. They listened to my directions but were still mystified by the prisoners.

I found a twig nearby, and looking directly into their eyes. I said, "Guys, this is what happens when you break Mama's rules," and I lightly tapped each one on the hand and slightly on their backsides—a simple chastisement. Then I said, "Now, look at those guys," and I pointed to the prisoners.

"When you break society's rules, this is what happens to you. Watch closely at how the young men are being treated. They're told when to move, when to stop walking, when to speak, what to do and not do—or suffer the consequences." We watched for a while in silence.

I explained why the prisoners were there and the difficulties they would be facing in prison. At the time, Titus was only eight years old, and he asked, "Why did they break the law? What about their parents?" I replied, "Some of them may not have listened to their parents who taught them right from wrong, and others may not have had good parents or lacked positive parental guidance."

The reason I took them to the courthouse was to demonstrate the consequences of poor choices, as well as to help them understand the importance of choosing good friends—people who make good decisions and share positive values and belief systems.

"Boys, when I say 'No,' there is a reason for my decision. When I set boundaries and curfews, when I give you chores and insist you always do your best and complete the task at hand with enthusiasm and pride, know there is a reason. I am teaching you the value of discipline and hard work," I told them. "We all have a good side and a bad side—you choose which to show. The young men you see today were not strong enough to say 'No' to their bad sides.

"Today, I want you to know that you have choices," I continued, "As you are introduced to society, understand that you represent your family. I hope you choose to make valuable contributions to communities you're involved in. Your personal story begins with making good decisions, and as your parent I am preparing you for your own life experience. I will do my best to encourage you so that you may offer greatness to your future society."

Several years later, when my eldest, Marcus, was in high school, he was part of a group of students who witnessed a female student being disrespected by other classmates. Those involved in the incident, including Marcus and the other witnesses, were summoned to the disciplinary principal's office. After speaking with the principal, Marcus was dismissed because the female student who had been harassed said, "Marcus was the only one who helped me."

On the way home from the meeting, Marcus turned to me and said, "Mama, thanks for taking me to see the guys in the orange jumpsuits. I remembered what you told us about mak-ing poor choices. I did not want to disrespect her." I replied, "Good job son. You did the right thing. Always work on mak-ing yourself stronger and becoming a better person!"

The Selfies

The Selfies: Self-Respect, Self-Knowledge,
Self-Esteem, Self-Confidence

In 2005, on our ride home from school, Julius stated, "Mama, if my hair were a little straighter and if my skin were a little lighter, I think I could make it." I asked him why he felt that way. He said he noticed that children with those traits were treated better. I was speechless but not surprised because through his lens, he was only processing people's feelings and how their viewpoints made him feel.

This assessment did not originate at home or from a family experience, but was something he innocently observed externally due to the unconscious mindsets of adults and his peers. I understood the viewpoint of my handsome 10 year old son of light medium brown hue, slightly curly hair. I also respected his resolve.

However, strictly due to his age but most importantly his environment, I felt that this phase of development would be short lived. Therefore, under my guidance, I allowed Julius to explore different barbers and hair styles and engaged in many deep self-awareness conversations. My goal was to transition him into self-actualization.

During this process of seeking self-knowledge, I thought about Doctors Kenneth and Mamie Clark's "The Doll Test." This test was conducted in 1940. It was administered to children between the ages of 3 and 7 years to determine how they perceived themselves.

During the test, students were given dolls of different colors. When asked which doll they preferred, children of both races consistently selected the white doll. The test concluded that "prejudice, discrimination, and segregation" created a feeling of inferiority among African-American children and damaged their self-esteem (NAACP Legal Defense Fund, Defend, Educate and Empower).

There is a saying: *"If you are white, you are right; if you are black, step back; if you are brown, stick around."* During the earlier years, this adage was embedded in the minds of Creoles and African Americans. In Alvin Morrow's book *"Breaking the Curse of Willie Lynch,"* he examines the science of slave psychology. Morrow explores this question and philosophy by connecting yesterday's history with today's progress then argues why today this mindset remains.

In one of my classroom discussions on diversity, I asked my students to include in their presentations personal encounters of discrimination and share how they resolved the experience and what lessons they learned. One of my student's spoke of how his great-grandmother favored her lighter skinned grandchildren over the darker skinned ones.

As this handsome, dark brown skinned, straight haired19 year old Creole spoke, I felt his pain and the stain of his great-grandmother's unconscious viewpoint—expressed to his mother's siblings—and the impact it left on his heart and mind about preference and privilege. In 2014, his great-grandmother died.

My student dearly loved his great-grandmother but the favoritism based on color of one family member over the other remains and the issue of who's better was left unresolved. Throughout my parenting practice, I never differentiated one son's color over the other but external forces introduced this discourse to my family.

No matter what culture one represents, early in a child's development, all families and institutions have the opportunity to positively shape the mindsets of the next generation of parents. Additionally, when it comes to brain development and issues of self-assessment, parents need to understand themselves and strive to improve their ways of thinking not only for the betterment of their children but of society as well.

For me, I practiced what I preached; I ruled with a pure heart, respected and honored all people, and taught my sons to do and know what's right. I helped them understand just because they have the right to do something does not always mean it is right. However, at the end of the day *"The fruit doesn't fall too far from the tree."*

Ways to Be...

During the time we preside over our children's development, it is imperative we not only guide them in the right direction, but also give them the tools necessary to make their own decisions. Helping your children navigate works hand in hand with the previously discussed advocate to advisor—first lead, and then gently advise as they develop the tools, skills, and attitudes you've nurtured so they may steer their own ships into success.

Ways to Be an Expert Navigator

- Talk to your child about your assessment of his/her skills, what he/she likes or dislikes, and his/her behavior and personality
- Create personal mental messages and daily inspirational quotes specifically designed for each child
- Talk to your child about your childhood, and compare and contrast yourself and your child
- Create an environment of happiness in a home that offers a safe place to retreat from unwanted outside influences, and teaches the value of such a place
- Show your children how to be responsible—based on maturity level—by giving them responsibilities
- Through modeling, show your children—at each developmental level—how to positively contribute and interact with society and various institutions, i.e., family, community, education, and religion

---

Supplemental Resources

- Suggested reading: *Screen-Smart Parenting* by Jodi Gold, MD
- Suggested viewing: *Finding Nemo* (watch shark chase scene before family viewing)
- Suggested listening: "I'll Be" by Reba McEntire, "Hall of Fame" by Will.i.am, and "Gonna Fly Now" by Bill Conti (morning wake up song)

Tell Your Story:

_____

_____

_____

_____

_____

_____

_____

_____

_____

_____

_____

_____

_____

_____

_____

_____

_____

_____

N: Navigation

127

*"Children are gifts to society;
what's your contribution?"*

—Lin Warmsley

Chapter 9

G: GRATITUDE

C hildren learn gratitude from our example. Children take cues from their parents on how to express thankfulness and show appreciation for their blessings and opportunities.

There are two pieces to teaching gratitude. Gratitude itself is a state of mind. It involves an upswelling of positive emotion in response to gifts, blessings, kindness, good fortune. Then there are good manners—the actions of a polite society. As parents it is our job to teach both. Feeling grateful is something that can be modeled. So can good manners. Ultimately we cannot force our children to feel grateful, but we can make good manners non-negotiable. Saying thank you shows respect and reflects an understanding of a kindness done or service performed.

The notion of "gratitude" holds power that can make or break a person's day. We all have the power to send someone soaring with joy with two simple words—"thank you." Teach this to your children. Make them understand the importance of expressing how grateful they are. Teach them to say thank you (good manners), but also remind them of the feeling behind the words—of genuine gratitude for someone or something.

Gratitude as well as manners are best taught by example. Let your children hear you thank others. Let them see you communicate your happiness when someone does something nice. Also, let them see you facing the world with a grateful heart, rather than bitterness about not getting "what I deserve." As we all know, children are copycats, and they'll replicate your outward gratitude just as quickly as they repeat bad words, and they will also begin to feel the truth behind those words of gratitude in their own hearts.

Try keeping a gratitude journal as a family. The idea of the journal—which Oprah Winfrey swears by—is to make a list each night of at least five things you were thankful for that day, keeping the family focus on what is good in the world, not the bad, what is working well, not broken.

Once you get into the habit of journaling each night, you'll find that your entire outlook on the world changes—you will spend your days looking for things to be thankful for rather than things to complain about. It's a fantastic exercise for anyone, but also a great tool for parents to teach their children how to look for the good parts of life.

Personal Story
The Road Trip

It was a hot, humid day in June of 2014, and I rented a car to travel to Texas to pick up my son from football camp. After driving for about five hours, the vehicle began to vibrate, the accelerator stuck, and the engine started to make strange noises. Startled and worried, I pulled over on the shoulder of the interstate.

Traffic was speeding past me, and most cars did not even slow down. However, one nice man on a motorcycle stopped to make sure everything was okay. He said, "I see your challenge. May I help you?" I accepted his assistance gratefully as I am not familiar with car mechanics. He attempted to figure out what was wrong, but he was unsuccessful.

He stayed with me as I contacted roadside assistance and arranged for a tow. After everything was in order, I thanked him. He said, "My mother would have killed me if I didn't stop to help you."

I told him, "Your mom would be very proud of you."

He replied, "I am so sorry I cannot stay with you until your service arrives, but I have to be on my way." I thanked him again, and he smiled as he drove off.

When Towaways Wrecker Services arrived to tow my car, I met Ricky and Tina. Tina was new on the job, and Ricky was training her. He carefully demonstrated how to secure the car into place on the tow truck. I was impressed by her apparent enthusiasm and work ethic as she was down on her hands and knees with Ricky following his instructions without question, all while wearing an eye-patch.

I found out she had sustained an injury at home, and when I asked her why she didn't take time off to recover, she responded, "Because I am new, and I want to learn the skills of this job. I enjoy what I do—helping people."

After a short and pleasant ride to the Lake Charles Enterprise rental office, I met with the rental manager and was given a new vehicle to complete my trip. I was further impressed by the way the manager, André, consoled me. He told me he was once in a similar situation with his children and everything worked out in the end.

He shared two of his grandmother's sayings—"When something starts out bad, it will end up good," and "Be thankful and grateful for every day and every situation, be it positive or negative, because the experience is all part of the life we live." I left with a thank you and a good-bye, and the rest of the trip went safely and according to plan.

Back in Baton Rouge, I shared my story with the Enterprise management, Brian and Demetria, when returning the car. Due to the car malfunction, they decided to wave all charges, and my rental was free! I thought back to my conversation with the manager in Texas— I guess he was right; bad situations do end up good.

After such a wonderful encounter with these helpful people, I decided to call Enterprise headquarters to report their exceptional service and to thank the management for hiring such great people.

However, I noticed a common factor in my encounter with all the people that helped me along the way— they all recounted memories of their families and quotes from their parents and grandparents, and they shared a spirit of gratitude for their lives, without dwelling on hardships.

That experience reinforced my belief that practicing good manners and modeling gratitude and kindness for our children leaves a lasting mark on them. Our natural instincts are to help others, and when those instincts are nurtured, lifelong, positive habits form.

Ways to be...

Gratitude is a deep feeling or state of mind. But even when we are in a bad mood, we must strive to be gracious, polite, and kind. Expecting gracious behavior from our children is essential for leading a happy life as a family. When your children first learn to speak, you constantly remind them to say "thank you," and the pride you feel when they finally say it on their own is overwhelming. We, as parents, must not forget to also thank our children for what they do for us, as we should never stop learning and nursing our relationships with them.

Ways to Be Gracious

- Approach life with gratitude and encourage your children to do so
- Teach your children to appreciate by praising them when they earn it
- Teach your children to be polite by modeling good manners
- Teach your children to be respectful by respecting yourself and others
- Teach your children to smile often
- Teach your children the principles of behavior and both positive and negative consequences of actions
- Show them the importance of volunteering and self-lessness by participating in community and volunteer events
- Help them master basic skills; nurture their passion; define their expertise

---

Supplemental Resources

- Suggested reading: *The Guide to Good Manners for Kids* by Emily Post and *The Gratitude Factor* by Charles T. Shelton
- Suggested viewing: *McFarland, USA*
- Suggested listening: "Grandpa Told Me So" by Kenny Chesney and "Dance with My Father" by Luther VanDross

Tell Your Story:

_____

_____

_____

_____

_____

_____

_____

_____

_____

_____

_____

_____

_____

_____

_____

_____

_____

G: Gratitude

> *"Train up a child in the way he should go,
> and when he is old he will not
> depart from it."*
>
> —Proverbs 22:6

Part Two

Chapter 10
Learning to Loosen the Strings

C hildren with good parents don't just get older—they grow up.
     This distinction is an important one, because personal development and emotional maturity are key components any child must have before truly becoming an adult. Kids take cues from every part of their surroundings as they become the adult they're meant to be, but the single biggest influence in charting a child's path to fulfilling adulthood is the guiding hand of a parent.

Parents who nurture their children's ethical conscious- ness and moral compass by observing their behavior cultivate children who have the proper tools for success later in life. However, time is of the essence, and the earlier parents begin working to ensure their children acquire these tools, the more likely they are to be successful.

I learned this lesson firsthand with my son Julius. From the ages 6 to 10, he was my constant companion on the college campus where I worked. It was a fruitful time for him as he experienced everything from classroom lectures to in-depth conversations with professors as he stood at my side.

But as is the case with any young man, he eventually craved independence. The summer he turned 11, he said to me, "Mama, this summer while you're working I want to stay at home because I'm getting older and I feel I'm old enough to take care of myself." It was something all parents eagerly await—a teachable moment.

Julius got his independence, but he got some responsibilities, too. Knowing that he was a good young man who communicated with me well, I allowed him to stay home on the condition he would complete a list of chores each day before I returned home.

Under this arrangement, he truly spread his wings. At the end of each warm summer day, he greeted me with his sparkling, joyful eyes and the list of jobs he'd finished while I worked. He thrived on being successful and fulfilling my expectations.

I could see him maturing before my eyes. We made a habit of ending our days with good conversation and cups of hot lemon tea, made by Julius himself. It brought us closer, and my pride for my son soared.

At the end of that summer, Julius said something that would make any mother's heart skip a beat: "This summer has been so rewarding to me," he said, his eyes twinkling like a toddler's. "Mama, I thank you for trusting and believing in me, because I feel so accomplished."

It was the beginning of a little boy's transition into the mature man I'm so proud to call my son. And the best part was that it was all his doing. I gave him my expectations and my guidance, but he's the one who realized his potential and sought excellence.

Twelve Years Later . . .

During September of 2014, I received a call from Julius that held an unexpected message. He said, "Mama, how can I say this? I mean no disrespect, but I hated growing up under your guidance because you were too mean, too strict, and too protective.

"But Ma, today, I am becoming a better person—a maturing adult who is focused on my goals, controlling my emotions, and understanding and caring for others. I am also learning from others, especially my coaches.

"I am calling to say *thank you*, because of your hard work in developing me, and to tell you how much I love you. You have prepared me for my future and daily I am applying one of your favorite quotes by Vince Lombardi: *'The only time success comes before work is in the dictionary.'* I just wanted to say thank you for the way you developed me and tell you how much I love you."

Holding back tears, I managed to say, "I love you too, son."

Supplemental Resources

- Suggested reading: *It Worked for Me in Life and Leadership* by Colin Powell
- Suggested viewing: Watch inspirational videos at www .motivationgrid.com
- Suggested listening: "A Mother's Love: Time Has Gone" by M.L. Revaz

What's Your Story?

_____

_____

_____

_____

_____

_____

_____

_____

_____

_____

_____

_____

_____

_____

_____

_____

_____

"As a man thinketh in his heart so is he,' not only embraces the whole of a man's being, but is so comprehensive as to reach out to every condition and circumstance of his life. A man is literally what he thinks, his character being the complete sum of all his thoughts".*

—As a Man Thinketh

Chapter 11
Foster Care
Quest for Independence

In a time of crisis, what happens when families are unable to take care of their children? What happens to the children? Who do these families turn to? There are two basic options when this happens. Either they ask other family members for assistance or these children are placed in alternative living arrangements called foster care.

Foster care is a state run child welfare system that provides childcare to families who are in crisis and unable to provide a stable living environment for their underage children. As a result of this legal guardianship agreement, these children become wards of the state.

Across the country, nearly half a million children are in foster care, fifty-two percent are males between six and ten; thirty-eight percent are females between the eleven and twenty. Additionally, data shows only 30.7% of foster care children graduate from high school and only 2.5% from a four-year college (Chapin Hall at the University of Chicago, Midwest Evaluation of the Adult Education Functioning of Former Youth Outcome at age 26, (2011).

When Ricky Richard was in the second grade, he lost both his parents—not from an unexpected illness or accident but from irresponsible and poor decisions made by his parents. Either they were young and foolish or hanging out with the wrong crowd.

After his mother went to prison, his father left Ricky and his four siblings with their grandmother. After seven years of unstable care, Ricky and his siblings were removed from the grandmother's home to his college age uncle's apartment.

Ricky and my son Julius are the same age. At the age of fourteen, under my parental guidance, Julius was planning for college, looking forward to a bright future and preparing to make extraordinary contributions to society. However, at that same age, Ricky was parenting his siblings while growing strong on his own.

FOSTER CARE CHILDREN IN THE U.S.	**408,425**
GIRLS IN FOSTER CARE PREGNANT BY 19	**50%**
FORMER FOSTER KIDS IN U.S. PRISON	**74%**
CARCERATED WITHIN 2 YEARS OF "AGE OUT"	**50%**
FORMER FOSTER YOUTH ON DEATH ROW	**80%**

Statistics provided by the U.S. for Children and Families, the US Department of Justice, the Casey Foundation and the National Foster Care Coalition

Personal Story
Growing Strong on Your Own
The Ricky Richard Story

Independence is a highly valuable and desirable quality for people of all ages. There is a sense of pride that comes with being able to accomplish a task without the help or assistance of another person. Most children slowly grow into their independence. Not without fear or hesitation, parents start to give their children small, simple tasks to complete, also known as chores, when their children are able to understand what it means to have responsibility.

These chores consist of cleaning their room, washing the dishes, or vacuuming the living room. These are appropriate tasks that help facilitate a sense of pride, independence, and responsibility in a child. Furthermore, as a child ages, parents begin to give their children more difficult tasks and responsibilities, hoping to instill within their children a deeper sense of independence.

All of this "adulthood grooming" helps young people prepare for adulthood. Parents are constantly planting good seeds within their children, which means that they pass on their knowledge, values, and wisdom in hopes that it will help their children successfully and independently navigate through the world around them. The ultimate hope is that one day those seeds will transform into a plentiful harvest.

Although most children gradually come to fulfill their independence with the help of their parents, some children do not have such a luxury. When I was eight, my mother went to prison. Shortly after that, my father, due to very complicated family issues, also vanished out of the family picture. And I found myself as one of those few, unlucky children. Being a foster care youth posed its fair share of challenges and obstacles, as one could imagine.

During my time in foster care, I was moved twice. I lived with my grandmother for seven years, but that was a very rocky time during my childhood as much of it was filled with verbal and physical abuse. After news broke out about the abuse, I was relocated to my uncle's home where I aged out of the foster care system. These situations, ultimately, led me into my independence early on in my development as an adolescent. As the middle child of five children, I had tremendous responsibility at home. Between helping take care of my siblings, cooking, cleaning, studying, going to school, and, when I turned 18, working a part-time job, there was little time left to enjoy just being a kid. I had to learn how to grow strong on my own.

Only 30.7% of children who grow up in foster care graduate from high school. Just 2.5% graduate from a four year college

Chapin Hall at the University of Chicago, Midwest Evaluation of the Adult Functioning of Former Foster Youth Outcome at age 26 (2011)

Choosing to grow strong on my own was just that: a choice. I made the choice to take responsibility for my own actions and life. At a very young age, I realized that if I did not make that choice my chances of being successful were very slim. I witnessed a lot of family members not make the choice, and their lives were not appealing, fulfilling, or purposeful.

For example, I chose to do things that would lead to my success, such as getting excellent grades, hanging out with like-minded friends, and finding good mentors. However, Lorenzo, my oldest brother, did not make choices that would help him rise above the unfortunate hand of cards he was dealt. Growing up he was a strong willed person, and I contribute much of my success to him because he was the strongest of my siblings. He was our protector.

Unfortunately, he tended to make decisions that were not in his best interest, and he was sentenced to nine years in jail while I was an undergraduate at Louisiana State University. My older sister Amber and I made the conscious choice to become successful, and we both went to college. We broke the generational curse by being some of first people in our family to attend college, and we could not be prouder.

Just as growing strong on my own was a choice, it was also a process. It caused me to constantly call upon my "selfies" (self-motivation and self-discipline), determination, perseverance, drive, and, most of all, courage. Many times I have been told that I could never accomplish a goal I had in mind, but I had the courage to pursue them anyway.

During my senior year in high school, I walked into my high school counselor's office to talk about a scholarship I wanted to apply for. It was the Bill Gates Millennium Scholars Program, a nationally competitive, full-ride scholarship given to 1,000 high school seniors each year. I was a very bright, promising high school student, graduating with honors and having served in numerous leadership roles within my school and community. I walked into her office with a sense of pride and confidence knowing that her affirmation and encouragement would inspire me even more to apply for the scholarship.

I asked, "Do you think I should apply for this scholarship? It's a full-ride to any university in the nation!" She swiftly replied, "I think you should focus more of your time on the local scholarships. I mean, those scholarships are really difficult to get and are not for students like you."

The sound of her words hit me like a brick wall. Here I was coming to her for affirmation and encouragement, and all I received was doubt and discouragement. For a split second, I felt dumb that I had even given myself the thought that I was capable or smart enough for such an honor. I began to doubt myself. I understood that I was a student at a K–12 school with a graduating class of only 43. Although close, I understood that I did not have a perfect GPA. I knew that far more competitive students with better GPAs and community service opportunities would apply. I knew that most of the recipients went to large public high schools. I knew that my chances of receiving the scholarship was less than 5%. I knew everything I needed to know about the scholarship.

All of those negative thoughts came rushing into my mind like flood waters clearing out all the positive thoughts I had before I stepped into her office. But as quickly as the negative thoughts came, they were gone, and what I was left with was the biggest drive and motivation I have ever mustered.

I learned in that moment that I did not need her affirmation or belief in me in order to apply for the scholarship. All I needed was to believe in myself. In the end, I would be the one writing the eight essays the scholarship requested of me.

After our conversation I would spend the next few weeks feverishly working on my essays. Most of the time, I would work on my essays after I got off from work at 9 p.m. and continue to work on them until 3 a.m. Then I would get up at 7 a.m., drive to school, and work on the essays until my classes started.

When I sent my application, I had written over 22 pages

worth of essays. I had invested countless hours writing and reviewing my work. Although not the smartest move, I had no one proof read my work in fear that the reader would again discourage me from applying. To others this may have seemed like a big gamble, but I did not want to think about it as a gamble because I had nothing to lose and so much to gain.

It was one of the best days of my life when I received notification that I was one of the 1,000 2011 recipients of the Bill Gates Millennium Scholarship Program (BGMSP) out of an applicant pool of 23,000. I graduated from Louisiana State University with absolutely no debt. The BGMSP is a 10 year scholarship, so I still have 6 years of funding I plan to use for graduate school. My life was changed forever by one envelope.

Imagine if I had let my counselor's discouragement be the deciding factor in my applying for the scholarship. I would not have any of the amazing experiences I have been given. There would have been no LSU or study abroad in Spain. There would be no hope in pursuing a graduate degree.

I do not think her words were intended as they came out nor do I think she understood their gravity or how, if I had let them, they could have affected the entire trajectory of my life. Honestly, I think she was trying to save me from failure and disappointment, which is something I had experienced a lot in life. But I have an optimistic spirit even if the chance of rain is 100%. That spirit is what kept me moving forward.

Sometimes you have to stay strong on your own. But no one is truly alone in their journey. During those trying times, I had the support of my siblings, family, mentors, family friends, educators, and my hometown community. You can stay strong on your own, but it is comforting to know that you do not have to seek out those who see the best in you and bring it out. Those individuals are the ones you should seek for friend-ship and refuge because there will come another day when the chance of rain is 100%.

Where are Ricky and His Siblings Now?

I asked Ricky to update me on where he is nowadays. He wrote me this update:

"After graduating from LSU this fall, I am attending gradu-ate school at George Washington University to obtain a Mas-ter of Science in global health with the goal of completing my doctorate. My older sister completed her undergraduate de-gree with a BA in elementary education at McNeese State University. One of my younger sisters is in her freshman year at McNeese studying psychology. My youngest sister is a high school senior."

Supplemental Resources

- Suggested reading: *Chicken Soup for the Soul* Book Series
- Suggested viewing: *Homeless to Harvard* and *Good Will Hunting*
- Suggested listening: "Needtobreathe," "The Script," and "Show Goes On" by Lupe Fiasco

What's Your Story?

_____

_____

_____

_____

_____

_____

_____

_____

_____

_____

_____

_____

_____

_____

_____

_____

Foster Care

> *"My Mother lied to me; she made parenting look easy!"*
>
> —Lin Warmsley

Chapter 12

Survivor

Parenting vs. The Odds

fter I graduated from college with a degree in journalism, I got married and began my family. I felt confident that I would be an excellent parent due to the phenomenal role models my mother and father were. Unfortunately, while I was building my nest, my husband and I began to develop domestic problems which eventually left me to fend for myself and my boys. The years following our divorce were extremely difficult for me personally and as head of household.

Transitioning from a two income household to a one income household was the initial and most impairing problem I faced. I was forced to make major financial adjustments like removing my sons from private school. Soon afterwards, I was laid off. It seemed as if one terrible thing after another kept taking our household by storm.

I was offered a new job; however, the hours were in the evening. Being away from my children in the evenings was not an option for me. At the time, my children were not old enough to stay home alone, and I could not afford a baby-sitter. For the next few years, there were days when I had to decide between buying milk for the family or gas for my car.

Especially in those moments, I remembered my mom

always telling me to have faith that good things will happen. I created and maintained relationships which assisted me and my family through hard times, befriending the workers at the local gas station who would allow me to run a tab when I didn't have enough money to pay for gas and the cleaners who would do the same with laundry and dry-cleaning.

I made the decision to take my career in a new direction—one that would satisfy me as a woman in the work force, and allow me to provide for my family. Whatever job I did would have to have normal hours, which meant I could mother my children. I sought substitute teaching, which provided a solution to the hours problem; however, the position did not provide any benefits and only lasted nine months of the year. I was blessed when a local realtor hired me to work part time, which stabilized my employment and financial situation.

Shortly thereafter, I landed a full-time teaching position at the local school. Always striving to better myself for my children, I enrolled in graduate school and earned a Master's Degree in Mass Communication, which allowed me to pursue higher pay-grade employment opportunities—such as teaching on a college level (Adjunct Professorship).

I eventually left the teaching position, moving on to a higher paying job. Although things were continuously improving, there were several storms we weathered as a family, particularly financially. When Julius was 8 years old, my salary was supporting my family, but due to my work-related travel, Julius's grades began to slip. I changed my job to care for his academic needs, and was laid off once again with four more months of tuition to pay for. This time, rather than removing him from private school as I had done in the past, I decided to sell my car to cover his educational expenses. After ten months of unemployment, I was returned to work with full compensation, which provided more than enough to purchase a new vehicle.

Through hardships, I learned the odds were stacked against me, and rather than feeling defeated and giving up, I became more focused. I learned the power of thought and constantly visualized my way out of difficult situations. These problems and hardships motivated me through the hard times, spurring me to greater heights.

Transforming negative situations into positive momentum was a skill I began to teach my children as soon as I could, for I knew they were sure to face adverse situations being the only African-American students in all white schools and neighborhoods.

My two young sons, ages 8 and 10 at the time, came home from school one day complaining they didn't like the way they looked. When I asked Titus why he wanted to change his color, he said, "Because when I raise my hand to answer questions, my teacher never calls on me, but all the time she calls on Tom, Dick, Mary, and everyone else. They never know the right answer, but I do!"

After having this discussion several times, I asked him to describe the students and his teacher. The students were all white and his teacher was African American. Rather than going to the principal, I used this situation as an opportunity to make my son mentally tough. I told him God selected him to represent a specific group of people, and He wants him to be proud of who he is. I encouraged him to keep raising his hand and prepare to answer questions when his teacher asks.

Towards the end of the school year, she finally recognized his raised hand. That day when I picked him up from the bus stop was a day I'll never forget. He was overjoyed with his accomplishment, and I was proud of his perseverance and mental toughness. That year, he passed with honors and was mentally stronger.

He entered high school—the only black student of 700 total students. In the first semester he encountered the "N" word. Of course, a fight ensued and both students were suspended for a week. Rather than pulling him out of school, I reminded him of the rewards of perseverance and mental toughness in pursuit of a goal.

Three years later, he was equipped with life's lessons and a $280,000 college scholarship. At the final basketball game, the students overwhelmingly embraced his accomplishments and sent him off with well wishes.

We learn to survive through challenges and grow through hardships. We must assume complete responsibility for the development and direction of our children's lives—even if that means making personal sacrifices. While my young family grew, I grew as well. At first, wearing the hats of both mom and dad was challenging and scary; however, I grew more confident in my parenting role, acquiring a sense of power rather than succumbing to the pressure and powerlessness. I chose to view problems as opportunities, and, by working through them, I became a better person.

Supplemental Resources for Overcomers

Suggested reading:
- Avery Canahuati:
  http://abcnews.go.com/blogs/headlines/2012/05/
  averys-bucket-list-five-month-old-girl-with-spinal-
  muscular-atrophy-dies

- Jamie Grace:
  http://www.projectinspired.com/musician-jamie-grace-her-story-of-triumph
- Leah Katz-Hernandez:
  http://www.ksdk.com/story/news/features/2015/03/27/leah-katz-hernandez-white-house-receptionist/70535138
- Maysoon Zayid:
  http://www.azcentral.com/story/entertainment/events/2015/02/24/muslim-comic-maysoon-zayid-fflasu-alma-mater/23870997

Suggested viewing:
- *Ray* with Jamie Foxx

Suggested listening:
- "Beautiful Day" by Jamie Grace, "Overcomers" by Mandisa, and "Break Every Chain" by The Digital Age

Tell Your Story: How Did You Meet Your Parenting Challenges?

_____

_____

_____

_____

_____

_____

_____

_____

_____

_____

_____

_____

_____

_____

_____

_____

_____

_____

_____

Survivor

Survivor

All parents are born; good parents are developed."

—Lin and Julius Warmsley

Chapter 13

Parenting Advice I
Fasten Your Seat Belt and Get Ready for the Ride

No matter how old you are when you become a parent, the job is a complex one. Your stage in life when you undergo that oh-so-important transition from "someone's kid" to "someone's parent" can make all the difference on how you parent, what kind of relationship you have with your child, and the impact of parenting on your life. Knowing a few things ahead of time can help.

Here's some general advice based on interviews with people who became parents as teenagers in high school, as twenty-somethings in college, and at thirty or over.

High School Age Parents

Becoming a parent essentially means becoming responsible for shaping the life of another. At times it can be difficult to direct our own lives successfully amid the chaos that surrounds us, and it's even harder to be responsible for both yourself and a baby who needs constant care and attention. It's by no means impossible for a high school student to be an effective parent, but the task is much harder without the years of life experience and perspective that older parents can offer their children.

But once a baby is on the way, there's no use in dwelling on what could have been if your bundle of joy had come later. Your primary concern is focusing on the little piece of you who will be crawling around the house before you know it. The key to being successful is understanding what parenting requires of you—chiefly time and money.

Being a high school student is time-consuming. School, work, friendships, community service, and other obligations eat away at your schedule. Being a parent on top of all that makes juggling even harder. It's essential to understand how many hours you'll have to commit to your child. The key is not only understanding that, but accepting it.

Your priorities will shift dramatically when you become a mother or father, so it's best to internalize that now and let go of the stress that may come with having to give up some of the things you'd like to be doing in favor of connecting with your child and also making a lifetime sacrifice to develop and love another human being.

Babies are also very expensive, which can be troublesome at a time when you're probably relying on your own parents for financial support. Start a dialogue with your parents about how this new arrangement will work. You'll need money for your child and someone to take care of your baby while you're in school, so plan ahead and be ready when your child is born. You don't want the joy of meeting your son or daughter to be marred by the anxiety of not having planned properly.

College Age Parents

The concerns of parenting during college are pretty similar to those of high school students. But college is a different animal entirely. It's a time when you'll get your first real taste of independence, and the opportunities are endless. College is a chance to learn who you really are and find your passion.

But so much freedom can be difficult to balance at first for some college students, and it's important for college-aged parents to realize that no matter what exciting opportunities come your way, *your child comes first.*

With a full schedule of class, work, and extra-curricular activities, time is always tight in college. But it's never too tight to make room for all-important time with your child. Realistically speaking, something will have to give so you can be there for your child. Your child's earliest years are essential because he or she is observing you and using those observations to inform an outlook and worldview. Absentee parenting is not an option, no matter how busy your schedule.

As you plan your days, prioritize the time you know your child needs with you. That goes beyond basic care, like providing food and clothing. Genuine quality time is of the utmost importance. It's not the responsibility of a day care or a babysitter to teach children essential life skills like manners and morals. That's a parent's job. Nor can a babysitter offer the unconditional love every child needs and deserves. Block out enough time each day to simply be with your child. It is in these casual, unplanned moments that you can make the most impact.

Money is, of course, another concern during college, a time of paying tuition, buying books, and possibly taking out loans. Your best bet is to budget thoroughly. Assess how much money you have coming in each month and determine your essential expenses. You'll likely have to cut out things you'd like to spend money on, like dining out, updating your wardrobe, or going out with friends. But rather than letting that upset you, understand that you're now serving something bigger than yourself and what is best for your child is paramount.

30+ Parents

Feedback from parents interviewed showed that age 30 and over is the best time to have a child. Older parents are not automatically better parents, and there are exceptions to every rule, including the one that says being older is being wiser. But parents reported that having children later in life allowed them to build financial stability and acquire wisdom that typically doesn't come in earlier years.

Older parents tend to have a more rich relationship with their children. Parents in their teens or early 20s can be too absorbed in their other responsibilities and the ongoing process of their own "growing up" to truly connect with a child. A flip side to that coin: young parents sometimes become more of a friend to their children instead of an authority figure, which can be troublesome during early stages of development. Older parents who are in stable relationships and have some degree of certainty about their futures can more easily strike the proper balance when interacting with their children.

Another thing that becomes easier with time is what one parent called the "I Want It Now Syndrome." Older parents are typically better at delaying gratification, controlling impulses, and taking time and care with weighty decisions. Knowing that your life is now driven by your children rather than your own desires makes it easier to make a thoughtful decision before taking action, rather than making rash decisions and dealing with potentially problematic consequences later.

Supplemental Resources

- Suggested reading: http://www.goodreads.com/author/ quotes/657773.Jim_Rohn
- Suggested viewing: "Is There Life Out There" by Reba McEntire (Music video)
- Suggested listening: Listen to TED Talks and Self Development audio tapes

Tell Your Story: Share Your Parenting Advice

Parenting Advice I

*No man should bring
children into the world
who is unwilling to persevere to the end
in nature and education.*

—Plato

Chapter 14

Parenting Advice II
Lessons Learned

*"Train up a child in the way he should go and when he is old he
will not depart from it."* (Proverbs 22:6)

God, Family, and Helping Others

The creation of families was God's idea. Therefore, it is natural for families to grow in faith together, especially with
young children. Children need to have a basic understanding of God's words.

If you foster this spiritual intuition at an early age, your
child will grow to trust his or her judgment. Fortunately, today's parents have enormous resources available to provide
appropriate spiritual guidance to prepare them for modern
society.

As a family, pray together. As parents, be good stewards, be
spiritual role models, and build solid relationships with families who share your convictions and beliefs;

Create a Family Mission Statement

"Parenting has not changed; society has." —Lin Warmsley.

Think of your parenting as footprints reaching into the future. You are walking a path your parents walked, or maybe

you have struck out on a new one. If you create a sense of continuity, the next generations of parents (your children, and theirs) will walk in your footsteps and continue the path. But parenting evolves—the footsteps don't stand still—they move onward. Creative and smart parenting is necessary to meet the needs of tomorrow's advancing civilization.

Today's parents need a clear strategy focused on child development as well as parenting empowerment. For example, your mission statement should start with the end in mind: (a) parenting empowerment and child positioning; (b) focus on your family's processes of understanding stages and phases of parenting and child development; (c) the goal to position each family member as valued supporters of as well as contributors to the family and to the next generation.

Create a Family Pledge

A pledge is a commitment to something that you promise to do. The goal of the family pledge is to teach family loyalty. One way to promote togetherness, trustworthiness, and thoughtfulness is starting each day with a pledge. Why not develop one of your own. Below is an example of a Family Pledge:

The Family Creed

I pledge to honor and respect my family,
my community, and most importantly.
I pledge allegiance to MYSELF.

I pledge to focus on becoming the best me
I am destined to be!
I pledge to become a valued contributor to society.

I pledge to plan and prepare for society's constant
evolution because I know it will change my perspective
and improve my world.

I pledge to be better, do better, and become the person
I am supposed to be.

I pledge to understand how I got to now with the goal
of bettering my family, the next generation,
and above all MYSELF.

Make a Promise, Keep the Promise

We've all heard these phrases: "A man's word is his bond" or "A handshake is as good as a contract." In today's society these words may have lost their meaning, but to a developing young mind they mean everything. In the eyes of a vulnerable child, trust is an emotional response, not based in logical thinking. A child expects you to keep your promise because that's all he knows.

For example, when Titus was 10, at some point during the school year I promised to enroll him in summer Karate school. Well, that summer I lost my job and could not keep my promise. He did not take Karate that summer.

Without clearly explaining why, I just removed that activity from the list but I did not think my not keeping that promise would deeply hurt him. Not until his freshman year in high school did I learn how that feeling of unhappiness and my silence remained heavy on his heart for three years. As we drove home one day, we talked about an upcoming summer activity he wanted to attend. I said yes, he could sign up for the event.

Looking me straight in my eyes, he said, "Mama, this time, please keep your promise". Baffled, I asked him what he meant. He reminded me of the Karate lesson and the promise I did not keep. After apologizing, I explained to him why I could not keep that particular promise. He said, "Mama, had you told me at the time, I believe I would have understood, but all these years, I felt you did not care."

When parents make a promise to a child, they must *keep it.* If the circumstances prevent your keeping your promise, explain. Make an effort to return to that promise in the future. Keeping your word models trustworthiness, which is fundamental to character building, and builds trust, which is vital to the parent-child relationship. When a promise is kept, use it as a teachable moment. Whenever a promise is made, use the mnemonic: *make a promise; keep a promise* to remind your child of the importance of being trustworthy.

Remain Positive but Plan and Prepare; Stay Focused on the Outcome

Be good-natured and stay focused on the outcome. Whether you are home or on an outing:

- Start each morning with a positive tone, and encouraging words of hopefulness and love
- Create customized mentalities for each child. When children have doubts about themselves, or their talents and capabilities, your message will resonate (*see Chapter 5, Personal Story: Creative and Endless Parenting*)
- Create a wholesome atmosphere of happiness.

As a result of proper guidance and mental development, your child will put away childish thoughts because at an early age and stage of brain development, he learned how to positively behave in various situations. Note that every situation will be different. Be creative and adapt and modify, but continue to learn, teach, and reach out.

Teach Your Children To "Do the Right Thing"

While in line at a local deli, I stood behind a young parent, around 30, with two kids—eight-year-old daughter and five-year-old son. As she completed and paid for her order, she turned around and we engaged in conversation. She introduced me to her children.

While the daughter was little reserved, her brother could

not stop asking questions such as how do I know his mom, did I work in the same office with her, did I have children—normal questions by a typical five year old. I continued a normal conversation with the family.

When I completed ordering my meal and the cashier gave me my change, I accidentally, dropped several coins on the floor. Hurriedly, the son fell to his knees picking up the change—I thought, "How polite." I planned to give him the change for helping me and displaying good manners until he said, "Oh, boy this is my money; I found it on the floor."

His mother scowled him then said, "You have money at home." However, he was refusing to hand the coins over to me or his mom. Again, his mother said, "Give the coins to me; you have money at home." It appeared that she had to convince her son that the coins did not belong to him. After forceful encouragement, he eventually returned the coins to me.

How do you teach your children to *do the right thing?* In the above scenario, what would you have done?

Parenting Strategy: Rule Number 1

Typically, doing the right thing is automatic for young children because they want to please their parents. However, young children learn to do the right thing by witnessing others modeling honorable and moral behavior. Psychologist David Kolb refers to this learning process as experiential learning which means the process of learning through experience, but it is just as easy to model wrong behavior as it is to model right behavior. Children learn by seeing and doing. Your parenting practice requires being cognizant of your behavior—by always modeling do-the-right-thing behavior.

Parenting Strategy: Rule Number 2

Children are extremely curious and their feelings are usually obvious. Daniel Goleman, father of emotional intelligence (EQ), believes learning how to self-regulate, caring for others, and learning how to interact with people promotes leadership development. However, from a parenting strategy perspective EQ nurtures, early on, the behavior of doing the right thing. Another strategy fostering moral behavior is using the Socratic Method by asking children questions about how would you feel if . . . or what would you do if . . . how do you feel about the decision you made. . . . This parenting strategy develops a positive mindset and also teaches children the importance of do-the-right-thing behavior.

Parenting Strategy: Rule Number 3

From the playground to the workplace, we often find one negative attitude that impacts the tone of the entire environment, i.e. one bad apple spoils the whole basket. Daily, we have the opportunity to make or break a person's day simply by positively, negatively, or neutrally interacting with them. Daniel Kahneman refers to this exchange as 20,000 moments. However, the brain only remembers the positive and the negative moments.

When you witness positive behavior from your child, give her/him a pat on the back, fist bump, high five, or sing the "Good Job, Good Job" song. The brain captures this image and will duplicate your positivity time and time again. This parenting strategy demonstrates, visually and enthusiastically, your approval of *do-the-right-thing* behavior.

The Rules: Show Them How to Play "The Game" Better than Anyone Else

Teach your children to be respectful to all and fundamentally teach them to respect and follow the rules. We live in a society governed by policies and procedures for the common good. Rules are designed for everyone to follow. However, when one becomes an expert in a field, it is time to study how others got to where they are. You can teach your children that by playing within the rules, while expanding and elaborating on common practice, they can be the best in their field.

Allow Them to Make Mistakes

Mistakes are inevitable at all ages and stages and they are teachable moments that can become lessons learned. For the child, mistakes can foster confidence and a sense of independence, as long as the child is not criticized for making them.

Believe it or not, mistakes are better made under your guidance. Even though the experiences are as painful to the parents as to the child, it is the experiences and lessons learned that stimulate mental growth and development. After all, mistakes provide on-the-job training—something every parent understands.

Nurture your child's curiosity

Remember the cliché "Curiosity killed the cat?" The saying originally meant "worry" killed the cat! Worry can kill you, but curiosity is vital and healthy for a person who wants to grow, learn, and achieve. Curiosity is a form of creativity that nurtures imagination. As parents, you have a unique opportunity to teach your child as Socrates taught his pupils by using the What, When, Where, Why, Who and How questioning technique (https://www.youtube.com/watch?v=wPINE_6cno8). This method encourages children to ask questions—always. It develops children's thinking skills and also helps them better organize their thoughts and goals. The purpose of the Socratic Method is to teach children how to communicate clearly and think on a higher level—ultimately becoming accomplished (*see Chapter 10: "Learning to Loosen the Strings"*). Helping your child get to where he or she desires to be starts with *you* and a parenting strategy.

When my children were young, they always asked questions—that's what children naturally do. At first, being a young and inexperienced parent, the multiple layers of questions were annoying until I learned the value of listening to my children. Acquiring the patience to listen to their thoughts, I began to appreciate their questions. I also learned more about their individual personalities and abilities.

For example, I noticed Titus's remarkable memory and his extraordinary innate commitment to achieving goals. I noticed the genius, sensitivity, and unbelievable physical strength of Julius and I noticed the strong-willed nature and compassionate heart of Marcus.

By listening to their questions I gained insight into how they were thinking and feeling. That insight better prepared me to guide their cognitive and physical growth. As a result of being open to a child's questions and curiosity, parents can develop a customized creative parenting strategy designed to map out a cognitive and physical growth development plan for their children. Therefore, when your child accomplishes one goal, instead of becoming complacent, he or she asks, "What am I going to do next"?

Nurture Your Child's Imagination

There are enormous benefits to nurturing a child's imagination. For example, imagination promotes the following: brain development, social and decision-making skills, the establishment of family values and beliefs, and problem solving (https://www .youtube.com/watch?v=FyAGxA386lI).

For a parenting strategy, start with the basics to cultivate creative thinking. Encourage natural (non-electronic) playtime and seek toys that promote innovative play. Watch your children unobtrusively, allowing them to use their imaginations to control situations and outcomes in their play.

My children were not introduced to the digital clock until they learned how to tell time on the analog clock; they were not introduced to the personal computer until they became proficient in handwriting. Today's families often favor the "what's happening now" syndrome and their children can miss some landmark developmental steps.

The world, as I've said before, is changing faster than ever. Families will benefit if parents set specific goals and limits on things like TV, electronics, and generally being "plugged in." However, it doesn't matter the time or decade, a recommended strategy for stimulating your child's imagination starts with the basics.

Appreciate Today; Be Glad about Yesterday; Be Grateful for Tomorrow

Communicate to your child that it is never too late to become what he or she is destined to be. By example show your child that every day on earth is a new day that should be valued and enjoyed; every day is a rehearsal to improve self; every day is a chance to experience and learn to become a better person than you were yesterday.

After All Is Said and Done, What's Left?

My sons grew up with these two philosophies in mind: "Do the right thing" and "Plan, prepare, and pray, then do your best, for God will do the rest." —Lin Warmsley.

My parents were determined that their children do better and be better than they—their goals were accomplished. However, parenting never ends. When our children are grown and on their own, it does not mean that our parenting job is done. They still need us.

Currently, my role is to be there for my sons and their future families. My grandchildren will be afforded extraordinary comfort that my children were only able to experience on a limited basis. It is their turn now to teach their children that nothing comes easily.

For now, because of their socio-economic status, I will encourage my sons to practice practical financial parenting so that their children "will learn how to live financially smart lives" (*President's Advisory Council on Financial Capability*).

Supplemental Resources

- Suggested reading: *Heaven is For Real* by Todd Burpo and Lynn Vincent;
- Suggested Web site: http://www.moneyasyougrow.org/; ellentube.com
- Suggested viewing: *Heaven is For Real*
- Suggested listening: "Survivor" by Reba McEntire

Tell Your Story: Share Your Parenting Advice or Strategy

Reading to the mind is what exercise is to the body."

—Joseph Addison

Chapter 15

Books

My Favorite Passion

My parents were eccentric regarding household reading materials. Newspapers, magazines, textbooks and The World Book Encyclopedia were the primary reading sources in our home. When we purchased the encyclopedia, we knew we were going to be the smartest kids in school and on the block. My parents told us that those reading materials would take us to places near and far without leaving home. They were right.

Later, in my teens, I learned that my parents limited the scope of what we read and saw on the shelves. They were protecting us from what they considered undesirable material. We never questioned their judgment.

My family subscribed to the local weekly newspaper, the Alexandria *Daily Town Talk*. Not only was the newspaper a source of current national, regional, and local events, but the Thursday paper was special because it included the weekend's grocery bargains and coupons. On Thursdays, after reading the paper, I helped my mom browse through it to coupon clip in preparation for Saturday shopping.

My most enjoyable memory was waking to the smell of freshly brewed coffee, bacon, and eggs and listening to my parents discuss current events. They were not educators but they held virtual Ph.Ds. in parentology, life processes, and child development. They also knew the importance of exposing us to experiences through the *World Book Encyclopedia*. From newspapers to recipe books to the encyclopedia, I don't recall ever seeing my mom without reading material in her hand.

My parents did not read us traditional story books but they reminisced and reflected on the past: childhood memories and family history. My parents modeled reading and storytelling to us. We acquired the love of reading through my parents' kitchen table chats over breakfast and the newspaper.

Based on their influence, I acquired a unique taste in reading real life stories. Although many fictional books hold deep truths, I favor non-fiction books such as the snapshot of my personal Legacy Library of books contained in this guide.

My book selection focuses on mental and physical development, educational research, goal setting, etc. My favorite book selection contained in this guide is a minuscule snapshot of my legacy that I am passing down to my children. I hope that they define what type of readers they are and that they will continue using books to guide them in their personal journeys as well as help their children acquire a love for reading and the learning process, as lifelong learners.

Supplemental Resources

Suggested readings:
- *You Can't Lie To Me* by Janine Driver
- *How We Got to Now* by Steven Johnson
- *Outliers* by Malcolm Gladwell
- *Blink* by Malcolm Gladwell
- *Mindset* by Carol S. Dweck
- *Breaking the Curse of Willie Lynch* by Alvin Morrow
- *The Road to Character* by David Brooks

Your Favorite Books:

Educational:

_____

_____

_____

_____

_____

_____

_____

_____

Informational:

_____

_____

_____

_____

_____

_____

_____

_____

Resources for Families:

_____

_____

_____

_____

_____

_____

_____

_____

_____

Fiction and poetry:

_____

_____

_____

_____

_____

_____

_____

_____

> *Movies are not mere entertainment. They sustain me and help me cope with my real life."*
>
> —Arlaina Tibensky

Chapter 16

Movies

My Other Favorite Passion

My parents' ultimate goals for their children were for us to speak good English, get a good education, and get good jobs. They were not educators but they were educated in life and its processes. They were extremely concerned about their children's choices and childhood development. They wanted us to be better and do better than they.

Knowingly or unknowingly, every activity we were involved in had an unwritten lesson plan, from shaping the choices we made in our lives and learning (and modeling) exceptional work ethics to developing a mental appetite for particular types of movies with teachable themes.

Sundays in our household meant early morning mass. After church, we regularly picked up a dozen donuts from Shipley's Donut Shop. Later that day we shared a family lunch then hopped in Nellie Bell, the family vehicle, heading to the movies. My parents exposed us to life and its cycles, in part through the magic of cinema.

Going to the movies was one of the favorite pastimes for me and my siblings. The movies we attended were often animated films with lessons in behavior management or social interaction, or family adventures. As we grew older, we watched movies with strong thematic or historical messages. At a young age, I did not realize the influence of these films and how their subliminal messages would impact my appetite for true-life movies.

As a result, today, I look at movies differently. I continued my parents' habit of movie-going after church. While today's themes and messages were quite different from my childhood experience, today there are more categories to select from. Learning from movies is truly a family affair.

However, I also exposed my children to all categories of movies, even ones with violence, drugs, and other depictions of harsh life. The difference in our movie-going was what happened after, and sometimes even during, the movie. We discussed the positive and negative impacts of the characters' decision making, their peer to peer influences, goal setting, and whether they stayed focused on their dreams.

I was an extremely involved and engaged parent and parenting solo was not easy. I searched for positive male role models for my sons through sports and their coaches. However, besides my father and their sports heroes, the male model that impacted them most was Denzel Washington.

My movie collection is saturated with Denzel Washington's stellar performances, i.e., *Glory, Unstoppable, John Q, Philadelphia, The Pelican Brief, Antwone Fisher, The Great Debater* and so many more. Of course there were other great actors we favored as well, such as Lou Gossett in *Officer and A Gentleman* and Samuel L. Jackson in *Coach Carter*. Though each of those movies was profound, Washington's roles defined the essence of character, confidence, and values.

As a matter of fact, when Titus went off to college at the University of Texas at Austin, I sent him a collection of movies to watch. When Julius was at Tulane University, 85 miles east of Baton Rouge, he was a fall season athlete and could not make it home for the holiday season. Therefore, every Thanksgiving while he was there, we met in New Orleans for dinner and a movie. My children share my desire for movies, books and music.

Dedicated to teaching my children lessons, I used books and movies to work with me. My parents did the best they could with what they had. So did I.

Benefits to Watching Movies with Your Children

Self-Assessment and Character Development

Movies can provide many benefits for both parents and children. When you watch a movie with your child, you share an experience together and expose him/her to another world and perspective. Movies can make you feel a whirlwind of emotions over the course of a rather short period of time, generating new thoughts and discussion. For parents especially, watching a movie can provide a short escape from the stresses of everyday life, as well!

Educational and Informational

Films that discuss poignant and delicate topics can provide a useful tool for teaching our children about social issues and empathy. When they see others struggling with and (hopefully) overcoming adversity, it provides a positive example for them to work through the troubles they will experience in life. They also will develop empathy for people in a wide range of experiences and walks of life.

Social Development

The theatre is a great date for young couples! When your child begins to show romantic interests, taking your child to the theatre with friends or a significant other is a safe, fun way to allow him or her to date while controlling the environment when he or she is still young.

Select Age Appropriate Movies

Brain research confirms that reading about, thinking about, or watching something happen has the same effect on the brain as when it is directly experienced. That's why so much learning can take place from immersing in a book or movie.

We all have experienced the adrenaline rush that comes while watching a thriller or suspenseful movie—as if we are in the midst of the action. As parents, we may forget to make time for ourselves and partake in activities that we enjoy. Watching an exciting movie can serve as a quick and convenient substitute for our hobbies and favorite activities when we only have an hour or two to spare! However, just because a movie is suitable entertainment for us does not mean our 11 year old child should watch it.

Relaxing

Comedies can provide an incredible pick-me-up if you are feeling stressed or down. They can also serve as the backdrop for a fun night in with the family and friends. There is nothing better than sharing a good laugh with the people you love.

Educational

Movies can inform and inspire. Many films depict the transformations of ordinary people into extraordinary heroes. They can be very influential. Inspirational stories can show different perspectives and pathways to greatness. They also provide wonderful examples for our children, showing them how hard work and big dreams lay the groundwork for an incredible life.

Emotional Development

There's nothing better for a broken heart than your favorite movie and a pint of Ben & Jerry's. Whether you or your child is experiencing heartbreak, watching a good movie together helps to take your mind off things for a while! In addition, as mentioned before, a thought-provoking or emotionally stimulating movie can spark empathy in a child, and require that he or she walk in another's shoes.

Family Time

Watching a movie can serve as an entertaining pastime and remedy for boredom. As parents, we often find ourselves in dire need for some R&R as well as kids saying "I'm bored!" and allowing them to watch a movie solves both problems. While satiating their boredom, a movie can provide an hour or two of peace and quiet for parents. Remember to discuss the movie with your child afterward to help him or her process the lessons and themes conveyed, or cope with difficult, confusing, or painful material.

Supplemental Resources

Suggested viewing:
- *Akeelah and the Bee* (2006)
- *Frozen* (2013)
- *Toy Story* (1995)
- *The Wizard of Oz* (1939)
- *The Wiz* with Diana Ross and Michael Jackson

Your Favorite Movies:

Movies That Taught You Something:

_____

_____

_____

_____

_____

_____

_____

_____

_____

_____

_____

_____

_____

_____

_____

_____

_____

_____

_____

Movies That Created an Emotional Response:

_____

_____

_____

_____

_____

_____

_____

_____

_____

_____

_____

_____

_____

_____

_____

_____

_____

_____

_____

_____

Family friendly movies:

_____

_____

_____

_____

_____

_____

_____

_____

_____

_____

_____

_____

_____

_____

_____

_____

_____

*"Music gives a soul to the universe,
wings to the mind,
flight to the imagination and
life to everything."*

—Plato

Chapter 17

Music
Yet Another Favorite Passion

When I was a child, my mother constantly listened to music. I would often watch her as she scurried around the kitchen swaying to the melodies. One day, I asked her, "Ma dear, why do you listen to music while you cook our meals?"

She flashed her signature half smile, then said, "Because it makes me feel happy, helps me work better, passes the time away, and also sets the tone of my spirit."

She used music to get us through each day, easing us into bed with smooth, relaxing music and waking us with spiritual music streaming from the kitchen radio. Music always helped me to begin and end my day on a positive note.

We loved to sing and dance as a family. Sometimes I'd stay up later than I was supposed to, in order to watch my parents dancing in the soft lamplight. I grew up listening to various musical genres from the soulful sounds of Ray Charles to the rhythm and blues of Stevie Wonder, and BB King, my mom's favorite, and Charlie Pride, my daddy's favorite.

Years later, my mother and I were at a restaurant, waiting for her favorite pizza. While we waited, I put a song on the jukebox—"Mama" by Boyz to Men. She looked at me tearfully, still wearing her signature smirk, and, for the first time, said, "I love you too, Linni!" It was my final tribute to her. Our final tradition we shared before she perished.

As a parent, I duplicated my mother's musical routines not only with my children but also with my nieces and nephews. Music helped me teach them self-control and order along with providing a healthy release for their excess energy. During weekend and holiday visits home, I invited them over for a *Soul Train Dance Line*. We listened to music for hours, laughing and dancing to the beats of "Thriller," "Beat It," or any of the most popular musical classics of the day.

As my children grew, our taste of music was similar but hip-hop, rap and other pop sounds were added to the musical equation. We agreed to share musical taste by listening to each other's favorite musical selections. As a result, my children learned the value of listening to various musical genres. Today, they continue to use musical selections to inspire and motivate them in their day-to-day activities.

Supplemental Resources

Suggested listening:
- K-Love Radio Station and "Smile" by Kirk Franklin
- Overwhelmed" by Big Daddy Weave and "America the Beautiful" by Ray Charles
- "National Anthem" by Whitney Houston at Super Bowl '91

Your Favorite Tunes:

Music That Inspires:

Music That Teaches:

Music That Makes You Feel Good:

"When times change, so must we"

—President Barack Obama
State of the Union Address
2014

Chapter 18

The Last Chapter
Change The Way You Think

"The only time you look back is to assess how far you have come."
—Anonymous

Sixty years ago, only 22% of women were in the workforce and nearly 80% of children under the age of 18 lived in "traditional" family households. However, this workforce data excludes working women representing Black, Asian, Spanish, and Native American groups. Although, typically, the agencies gathering such statistics tend to overlook them, Black women have always participated heavily in the work force while raising their young children.

Today, the participation of women of all ethnicities in the labor force has tripled and fewer than 50% of children under the age of eighteen live in traditional family households. As far as fathers are concerned, today they are more engaged in the role of parenting, from participating in household chores (beyond the traditionally "masculine" role of home repair) and sharing childcare responsibilities to raising children alone in a single parent household. This contemporary family demographic is a normal cultural progression.

So where we are today is different than where we were even 20 years ago, let alone in my parents' day. Some things to consider:

- 80% of Americans coming to maturity today will become parents
- The role of the father is evolving in positive ways
- The parenting role of women has not changed much, though more and more women are working than ever before
- The world as we know it is changing more rapidly than at any other time in recent history
- It is more important than ever for everyone to work together to raise the next generation of parents

We are all in this job together, i.e. black, white, brown, and yellow. Mothers need to remember that the fathers of today are continuing the journey of their fathers in redefining the role of "dad." Moms can help dads find success as hands-on, nurturing, thoughtful, proactive parents in full partnership with them. And it will serve fathers to remember that mothers have a cultural history of, in many ways, solo parenting. Even in households where both parents worked, it was the mother who took on the lion's share (or should I say lioness's share) of the day-to-day parenting duties.

There is an old saying, *"When you teach a man, you teach an individual but when you teach a woman, you teach a nation."* It reflects the fact that the weight of parenting traditionally has rested on the shoulders of mother. (There are always exceptions to any rule!) Parents of both genders are well served, today, by respecting where the other is coming from and working together to form a more successful, enlightened partnership for the betterment of the children.

My mother made parenting look easy. Though parenting is inspiring, it is a difficult job. Today, parenting is even more demanding as both parents are increasingly in the work force, and there is less community support for parents as the extended family is becoming a thing of the past. Also, parenting requires more attunement with other cultures as our society becomes increasingly multicultural and global.

As society advances, parents are better served if they change the way they think about how to raise the next generation of parents—especially when it comes to preparing them for an unknown tomorrow. For example, at an early age, in other countries, children are taught multiple languages as a means of survival. Because they have transferable communication skills, they are better prepared for a changing world and demanding employment landscape. We lag behind in this area.

Why is Europe, for example, less ethnocentric than we are in the U.S.? Part of it has to do with the multiplicity of languages on one continent. As people traveled across borders, the need to understand different languages was part of their daily living—their normal. As I mentioned, Titus played professional basketball in Europe.

During the on and off seasons, he traveled to other countries. Although his primary residence was Germany, I encouraged him to learn other languages. Driving from Berlin to Paris is like driving from Baton Rouge, Louisiana to Austin, Texas. While there, he learned three languages fluently and understands a few others. Today, he lives in a small German town in Texas. Image that. Who knew?

In America, English is the dominant language but my mother did not speak English skillfully. However, had my mother understood the concept of global language and understood the long term benefits of knowing multiple languages, she would have certainly ignored the insults she experienced as a child of French-speaking parents and I would be bilingual today.

But she (and her parents) lacked insight of a global tomorrow because her era was less global with limited mobility. Her world did not move as fast as my tomorrow but she did her best for us equipped with the parenting knowledge passed down from her parents. This example of prioritizing language acquisition is simply one of many ways that today's parents can and should think outside the parenting box built by earlier generations. Years past, families and communities band together for a common goal. Today, as parents, we need to expand our understanding of the world and of the needs of our children's tomorrows.

"You packed their bags, what's in their luggage?" The foundation of parenting teaching starts with a strong moral compass. How are you preparing yourself to make better contributions to society? Are you ready to learn more about how to raise the next generation of parents? What are the main challenges of today's and tomorrow's parents?

Parents face numerous challenges: parents compelled to work long hours; parents as well as children adjusting to separate households/co-parenting/stepfamilies; timely introduction and integration of technology and its virtual influences; increased peer pressure; unsanctioned and careless cyber behaviors; negative influences from the media and the lack of common parenting practices or creative parenting strategies.

Today's parents are living in a highly technological and fast-paced society that requires parents to keep up with societal changes or their children will be left behind or develop a distorted sense of reality.

In your parenting strategy, how do you measure up? Do you agree or disagree:

• Parents want their children to live in a better world.
• Parents want their children to be happy and successful.

- Parents should keep up with modern technologies.
- Parents should take advantage of available educational opportunities and resources.
- Parents should work together creating common practices for the good of our future society.
- Parents need a family plan of action.

Deciding how you feel about the above questions is the first step to creating your own parenting plan of action. Your own parenting moral compass is how you will figure out how to proceed as a parent, as a co-parent, and as part of a community of parents.

"Old fashioned" parenting can be a good thing but today's parenting practices require broad and creative mindsets. Best practices probably involve learning from the past but then connecting that with the future, so that they are suitable to the times in which we live, with the goal of achieving favorable results.

The basis of your parenting journey starts with your prior parenting influences which encompass not only your parents' but your co-parent's parenting philosophy as well. But there is always more—much more—to learn!

You believe in the value of education. You encourage your children to go to college. So think of your own education as a parent. As far as your personal parenting journey goes, think of parenting as a discipline acquired through levels of knowledge.

Look at your parenting education as a sequence of hard won degrees ensuring your expertise in the field. For instance, if you are parenting children or a child between the ages of 0 and 9 years of age, you are working on your Bachelor of Science or Arts degree. Normally, it takes three to five years to complete a bachelor's degree—that's it. A bachelor's degree in parenting takes twice as long—up to 9 years to complete.

A parenting course of study is a lifelong learning experience of discovering, teaching, coaching, and understanding numerous ages and stages of child development. This undergraduate curriculum encompasses the following stages of child development: infants to toddlers/preschoolers to school age children. Your goal is to understand how your children develop and successfully move through each phase.

If you are parenting children or a child between the ages of 10 to 18 years of age, look at this part of the journey as the first part of your graduate studies. You are working on your MS or MA. Before pursuing a master's degree, students are often required by universities to take a test referred to as the GRE (Graduate Record Exam). However, for you, there is a parenting entrance exam to enhance your parenting journey (course work) and I like to refer to it as the GRP (Grandparents Retirement Plan)!

This exam addresses, reviews, and confirms specific parenting strategies. It also supports you as you continue to build and modify your knowledge with the goal of developing healthy children and above all a healthy and guaranteed retirement package for grandparents (the GRP).

In their graduate course of study, parents build on connecting today with tomorrow, just as our parents did, but with even greater challenges to face as the changes happen so much faster now. It is also when parents confirm the moral compass, check emotional control (the parents'), and teach teens how to manage their emotions, understand how to deal with teenaged pressures, understand the scope of teens' mental and physical growth and their issues as they grow and develop into young adults.

And if you are parenting a young adult or adults over 18 years, you are earning a doctoral degree and no doubt working on your dissertation in *Parent-ology*. By definition, a doctoral degree is the highest level of educational attainment. Most institutions place a timeline on completing a PhD.

However, there is no timeline of completion regarding developing children or their education and empowerment. Child-drearing is a lifelong quest. Even at a later age and phase, children still need their parents as their Personal Consultants or Confidential Assistants.

After all, the brain does not completely develop until twenty-five years of age. After researching rats, Jean Piaget and B.F. Skinner initiated research on children. Skinner's research focused on behavior while Piaget focused on cognitive development. They found that the brain develops well into adulthood and that certain areas of the brain, such as the parts that help us make reasoned decisions, develop last.

From the naming of your child to the development of his/her mindset to the making of his image, what you do now and how you parent your children will impact them for the rest of their lives. As you already know if you are a parent, your life changes when your child is born. It is no longer just about you. It is about your child, your family.

Today's parents cannot afford to leave their children's development to chance. Parents have an amazing opportunity to "pass the truth to the next generation. . . . Teach them early, what we learn late." —Noella Bleu. What can you do to contribute to the science and art of parenting? Parenting skill sets are transferable. It's your legacy. Each generation will make a contribution to society, including yours.

Supplemental Resources

- Suggested reading: *A Whole New Mind: Why Right Brainers Will Rule the Future* by Daniel Pink and *7 Ways You Can Change the World* by Monica Bourgeau
- Suggested listening: "Rise Up" by Andra Day
- Suggested listening and viewing: "Black or White" by Michael Jackson
- Suggested listening and viewing: "We are the World" by Michael Jackson

About the Author

Lin Warmsley, parenting strategist and coach, dedicated her life to a twofold mission: to develop children and raise good parents. She's combined years of research and her invaluable experience as a mother of three to create How to Raise Good Parents, an all-inclusive guide to help others become the best parents possible.

After divorce left her to build a family on her own, Warmsley chose to rise to the occasion, raising three sons who have collectively earned more than $1 million in college scholarships. She attributes much of the success with her children to observing the tactics of her own parents.

Warmsley earned her BA in broadcast journalism from Louisiana Tech University, an MA in mass communication from Southern University, and initiated doctoral studies in human resource education and workforce development at Louisiana State University.

What Are People Saying about Lin?

From parents to students to organizations, here's what clients are saying about Lin:

Parents

Thank you so much for all of your help and support. While I do feel that our daughter was ready to make certain changes and that she definitely has natural ability and intelligence, I do not know if she could have achieved her goals this semester without you. Your constant presence and encouragement kept her on track. I thank you for helping her to achieve her dream and goal of making FABULOUS grades this summer session.

    Nelson and Sally

My daughter was going to be extremely far away from home and as a parent I was filled with great apprehension. You helped ease my mind. You gave me your time, knowledge, understanding of natural parenting, and these are what I needed to feel okay about letting my daughter go to another state to attend college. Thank you so much for your parenting support.

    Katy

I just wanted to take a moment to say just how much Kathy and I appreciate ALL the good work you've done for our son in helping him attain academic achievements which have been so important to his college life. I'd venture to say that his success would be noticeably less without your intervention and input (and strong efforts to keep him focused on his goals).

Chip and Kathy

I wanted to thank you for your work with my daughter. After a series of events that left her lacking confidence, rebellious, and with an attitude that only a parent of a 16 year old would understand, you were able reach in and bring out a young lady that I am proud of today.

You showed her that confidence comes from within, organization is necessary, and that you can achieve anything you want if you first believe in yourself.

I feel as a parent I worked on these skills each and every day but sometimes it takes someone other than a parent for a child to embrace the teaching. I am truly grateful for your ability.

John

Students

I am so appreciative of you. You changed my life. I will never forget you.

Miranda
Former student

You kept me grounded. You were my inspiration. Because of you I made it to college. Thank you!

Katelyn
High School student

Organizations

Ms. Warmsley has the capacity to establish an outreach program, inform audiences on certain issues, educate and motivate people to take action. Ms. Warmsley speaks and shares information from personal experience, as well as reporting on current research.

> Judy Mabry
> Program Manager
> ESEA, Chapter 1

Lin Warmsley shares effective strategies and helpful ways that parents can successfully assist their children with homework. She was able to communicate with the parents using a grassroots approach, as she shared the peaks and valleys of raising three sons as a single parent. The audience could relate very well to her personal experiences and applauded in agreement throughout her presentation.

> Dianne Helaire
> Principal

Ms. Warmsley is a dynamic speaker who really knows how to hold an audience and motivate that audience toward self-improvement and the improvement of others. I recommend Lin Warmsley if you are in need of a fine presenter, especially in the area of parenting education.

> Lee M. Faucette,
> Former Director Federal Programs

How to Raise
Good Parents

All Parents Are Born,
Good Parents Are Developed

Lin Warmsley

To order direct write to:

How to Raise Good Parents
P.O. Box 5223
Baton Rouge, Louisiana 70821

Made in the USA
Lexington, KY
15 January 2017